EVIL'S GOOD
BOOK OF BOASTS AND OTHER INVESTMENTS

by

Simon Cawkwell
(aka Evil Knievil)

First published 2002

ISBN   0-9542748-0-6

Published by t1ps.com Ltd
PO Box 36641,
London SE1 4XN
Tel 020 7604 4856

Cover design: Emma Cawkwell
Cartoons: Roger Leboff

Printed by SMP Group plc
Units 217 C&D Swan Road
Westminster Industrial Estate
Woolwich, London SE18 5TT

CONTENTS

Introduction - By Tom Winnifrith

The first time that I encountered Evil Knievil was when, as a younger and thinner journalist on the London Evening Standard, I tipped some piddling Ofex listed technology company. It was a great stock: strong balance sheet, bulging order book, amazing technology. The only thing wrong was that this bloke Evil Knievil was shorting it and its shares were not going up.

Of course Evil had done some amazing homework and established that the man running this company was quite simply a compulsive liar. So the balance sheet was a complete work of fiction as were the orders and the technology did not work. I learned my lesson. Even if you know you are correct, never cross swords with the Great Bear.

Subsequently, Evil, aka Simon Cawkwell, became a good friend. We come from rather similar backgrounds. His father (a great classical scholar and rugby player) lectured to my father (also a classical scholar) at Oxford. Neither Evil nor I are quite that academic. Oddly, both our fathers are not really that interested in money nor how the City works. Greats men have greater matters to consider.

When stockmarket editor at UK-iNvest I managed to secure a column for Evil. Within a few months Evil had already received lawyers letters from two companies. Of course he was correct in what he wrote and neither company had a leg to stand on. The management of UK-iNvest did not take such a view. Racking up their costs by hiring expensive, but weak, lawyers they decided it was simpler to sack Evil than to make a stand. UK-iNvest was run by cowardly incompetents.

Evil immediately found himself working against UK-iNvest for the late lamented thestreet.co.uk but we remained friends. He is a man of great loyalty who always does what he says he will do. That, and his ability to enjoy life and to laugh at himself makes him great fun to work with. He is generous to a fault. If the apprentice rather than the sorcerer comes up with a good shorting idea he will always give credit where credit is due.

Evil can easily be mistaken for a slightly inebriated buffoon. When recording our fortnightly EvilCasts on our website t1ps.com, at least once a month he will admit to buying £50,000 worth of some stock which I have never heard of and which he will never understand. "What does it do?" the apprentice asks. "Er... No idea but a bloke told me to buy some" chortles the sorcerer. Inevitably Evil's forays into monoclonal antibodies or WAP technology end with him handing back a small portion of his other gains.

But what is the odd £50,000 loss to a man who can make £250,000 in a week. One Cheltenham week a friend encountered Evil on the Friday and asked him how he had fared. Up £8,000 came the reply. It later emerged that Evil's balance on the horses had swung from plus £50,000 to end at minus £2,000 but that he had just trousered £10,000 on the Friday night betting on a third division football match. Proof that at least something good has come out of Mansfield Town.

There is of course a very serious side to Evil away from his gambling and his stockmarket punts. This is the man who was the first to unravel the accounting frauds perpetrated by Robert Maxwell. This is the man who pointed out the flaws in the accounts of Tiphook before it collapsed. The standard of City analysis of these – and so many other – matters was, and is, painfully bad. Men like Evil are needed to put some balance into proceedings.

Recently Evil and I sat down to look at the accounts of Ispat NV, a steel company greatly favoured by the British Government for £125,000 different reasons. Wall Street analysts and both the FT and the Economist had lavished praise upon this company and its chairman Mr Mittal. The British Government assured its counterparts in Romania that it was a company of good standing. Yet it took Evil just a few hours to see that this company's depreciation charge looked seriously odd and that its off balance sheet debts were not insignificant. While the analysts, journalists and the British Government must have spent weeks arriving at the conclusion that this company was a jolly good bet, within less than a day Evil had established that its net worth was, at best, not a lot more than nil.

As we sit in Evil Towers every two weeks recording our EvilCasts for t1ps.com one can sometimes forget what a brilliant forensic mind is sitting opposite you. But the reminders are regular. At least once a month Evil will quite simply pull to pieces the accounts of some company or other. In the space of five minutes you know that you never want to own that stock. This is surgical demolition.

If I said that editing Evil's book was an unmitigated pleasure I would be telling a Stephen Byers. In removing the obvious libels I have shortened this volume by a good two or three pages. Reading this book once the editing was complete has been a thorough pleasure. It is not only highly amusing but it is also a complete education on how the stockmarket really works. I cannot recommend it too highly.

EVIL'S GOOD
BOOK OF BOASTS AND OTHER INVESTMENTS

I dedicate this book to fraudsters and, of course, gullible people everywhere without whom there would be no bid to hit.

A short note about the cover of this book:

I chose the graph of REGUS since it is a perfect example of how to make lots of money quickly (£100,000+ in this case). As you can see, it was not that easy to start with. Instead of going down it went up. That's the power of Merrill for you. I had noted Regus as a possible flotation the year before it plummeted, 2001. The flotation was pulled – always a suspicious sign. But, a year later, when I looked at the proforma balance sheet I fell about laughing and thanked my lucky stars that so many people are born stupid.

The Front and back cover of this book were designed by that talented young designer Emma Cawkwell, a.k.a. little Evil.

The cartoons within this volume were produced by Roger Leboff - a man whose cartoons at one stage made HSBC James Capel's research worth reading.

Thanks are due to my team of proof readers: Danby Bloch and Tim McNally from t1ps.com; Sarah Thomas (aka Mrs Tom Winnifrith) and Dr Tom Winnifrith whose mother appears on page 10, whose son appears frequently in this book and who himself spent many a happy day listening to my father lecture.

For an up to date briefing one the latest thoughts and activities of Evil Knievil there is only one place to go. Evil opens his diary once a fortnight in the EvilCast webcast (also available in transcript version) on the Internet site www.t1ps.com

Like Colin Blackbourn, Nigel Wray and others Evil also posts regularly on the t1ps.com bulletin board.

A BEAR'S BACKGROUND

"Give us this day our daily bread.
And forgive us our debts, as we forgive our debtors.
And lead us not into temptation, but deliver us from evil"
- The Book of Matthew, chapter 6 verse 9 (also, plausibly, Robert Maxwell)

My parents arrived at Oxford from New Zealand in latish 1946. My father came on a Rhodes scholarship and having picked up a respectable degree walked a hundred yards from Christ Church to become a don at University College in 1950. He is still there but is now an emeritus fellow. I think he gets dining rights but has nothing to do with the administration of the place. Nothing whatsoever about his conduct in or attitude towards life has anything to do with gambling. He is about as financially risk averse as it is possible to be. I do not know why. His aversion may be genetically derived or it may come from a childhood in the thirties where he saw at first hand the consequences of a deep and sustained depression. My mother has virtually nothing to do with money and, save in the practical sense of recognising it as a means of exchange for life's necessities, has absolutely no interest in the subject whatsoever. I have never once heard her raise it as a topic of conversation and, although she has not said so, I think she thinks the subject pretty boring and a mark of inferiority on the part of the speaker if raised.

My father's second name is Law. This is rumoured to be because he, and thus I, are descended from John Law, the Scottish financier who set up the Mississippi scheme and was generally in charge of financial scams in France in 1720 (he might have operated the South Sea Bubble here at the same time but for being wanted on murder charges). So there's a hint as to my interest in financial markets. That said, there is absolutely no evidence that John Law has anything to with my family whatsoever. Anyone got a pocket DNA kit to take to John Law's grave in Venice? Cash paid.
I was born in 1946 and brought up in north Oxford in what I now recognise were virtually idyllic conditions – only, needless to add, I did not even begin to realise it at the time. The place was stuffed with kind

enthusiastic intelligent and honourable people. My contemporaries had parents who had been through the war. They did not complain and they put their backs into getting things done. So, although there was not a lot of cash around, all was always provided for in the most stimulating and equitable environment any child could conceivably wish to be born into.

Aside from a rather handsome married vicar who publicly canoodled with a woman who was not his wife, I never heard of any hint of marital infidelity in my childhood Oxford. Divorce was regarded as socially inferior.

The Dragon School, on the banks of Oxford's river Cherwell, was heaven for young boys and, as far as I am aware, so remains. It was also an establishment where Tom Winnifrith's grandmother distinguished herself playing rugby. Although I am the son of a don and was therefore expected to shine in the academic department, I did nothing of the sort. Only occasionally could I be bothered to put in any sort of effort. So I was eclipsed by the swots. And, given that one or two of the swots were clever fellows into the bargain, the eclipsing was pretty thorough and, worse, persistent. I do not know what would have happened had I gone to a school where my contemporaries would have been less able. But I suspect the result would have been much the same.

The only activity in which I excelled was target shooting and was told by the shooting master that I was the best he had ever trained. I think it may have been because I was quite tall for my age and, having a good eye, obtained the same picture round after round and squeezed gently through. It led to consistently high scores. The shooting master gave me a letter of introduction or something like that for me to hand on to the captain of shooting at Rugby, my next school. On arrival and quite understandably I took along my letter of introduction and, on being tested alongside members of the Rugby shooting eight, trounced or equalled the lot and I asked when I would be admitted to the eight. I did not know that thirteen year old boys are not supposed to talk like this.

As it happens I never made the eight since I developed a flinch when using .303 rifles as the kick forced the thumb of my left hand smartly into my cheek – I am a left-hander. I assure you that if you do this for long you will develop a bruised area and you will flinch each time you pull the trigger. This is not good for scores. I presume that the butt of my rifle was just too short for some reason. By the age of fifteen I had lost all interest in shooting – and this despite having terrorised every bird in north Oxford over the previous five years.

I went to Rugby because my father had been capped in the sport of the same name for Scotland. He argued that I would be sufficiently tough for the game – my brother went to Shrewsbury since he was and is less physically robust than I and thus more suited to soccer. But I am basically effete or, if not that, indolent and I have never played rugby since I left school. I may have watched twenty games – almost all on television and as a result of a bet. So much for my father's hopes by way of sporting prowess.

The summer game was of course cricket. My father played for a variety of teams. There were the Barnacles, the Academics, the Cryptics and others who were rather posher. I heard names such as I Zingari and had various ties pointed out to me. Goodness me, that world has changed. Nobody under fifty today wears a club or school tie. Yet, when I started in the City, Friday was always a club tie day, particularly school and regimental ties. I cannot say that this change matters. It is just a fact.

My family's aged Vauxhall Wyvern would trundle to village cricket grounds all over Oxfordshire and neighbouring counties. I can't readily remember the names of the villages now. But, to my mind, the best ground was that of Cookham Dean. It was so small that sixes were easily scored. Those matches were followed by invitations to the nearby house of a wine wholesaler based on Paddington Green. My father then used to buy wine for University College and I well remember the merchant's elegant labels on the occasional half bottles that were given to my father as samples by which to encourage trade. Curiously, given that I must drink more wine per annum than anybody else in London and, for all I know, the universe,

I did not take to wine until I was approaching sixteen years. That said, I have been making up for those lost years ever since. The drawback has been that, since I am what is referred to in the animal husbandry business as a good converter, I turn those excess calories into fat.

When I was eleven I broke bones in both feet during the Easter holidays. Thus the following summer term's cricket was a complete write off and I never really regained a personal playing interest and hardly ever watched a match of any sort. But I attended a number of matches at Lord's when I lived in St. John's Wood in the early nineties and a few years ago took a bit of a swing at betting on them. The result has been that I now think test match cricket is extraordinarily interesting. What seems such a slow game in fact fluctuates enormously – sometimes in the space of a few balls. And, whilst I will never understand what those crafty bowlers are preparing, I enjoy having it explained to me after they have done it. (Some people do not enjoy cricket. And the most prominent opponent of the game of whom I am aware was the late Lady Menzies, whose husband, Sir Robert, was Prime Minister of Australia. She observed that she had been to a cricket ground and had visited it twenty years later only to find that the same two batsmen were still at the crease.)

To start with, and for a fortnight a year during the summer holiday, my family rented a cottage by the sea, typically in Cornwall or Wales. This entailed Walls plain vanilla ice cream, rock pools and sand between one's toes along with brief dips into cold seas – global warming had yet to arrive. For myself, I can't get enough global warming.

However, and later on as I entered my teens, my family went to the Lake District and a house set above Lake Buttermere. These holidays involved walking up hills and back down again. I never enjoyed this since, although I appreciated the view from the top, I did not think it especially interesting to walk up hill – it seemed as pointless an activity as that undertaken half the time by the Grand Old Duke of York's ten thousand men.

That said, I went on long walks around Lake Buttermere and its environs and have never lost an interest in watching water and fishing. Those days out must have entailed covering comfortably upwards of fifteen miles at a time. Thus I always thought marches of (say) three miles when I was in the corps at Rugby entirely pathetic attainments. I suppose that Rugby's point was that a high proportion of my then contemporaries came from the soft South East where not a lot of walking was done at all.

Regrettably, I have not continued with fishing. My addiction to gambling and the market rather pathetically does not let me lift my eyes from the screen. Save for lunch, I suppose. That said, I have taken fishing quite seriously: for instance in 1969, my wife and I left Lusaka at 5.00 a.m. one day and arrived perhaps two hours later under the shadow of the Kariba dam. This mighty enterprise chewed fishes through its turbines with the result that all variety of predators waited below to take the ready-chopped harvest. One of those waiting proved to be a tiger fish, which may have weighed about ten pounds. It elected to pursue my spinner. It fought ferociously and had fearsome teeth. I think I chucked it back – I could see no future in cooking it.

But it was a hot day and, since I had seen a Rhodesian bush ranger type swimming around with a spear gun and wearing, as it happens, a black Stetson (I can't think why he had it on for swimming – however, it certainly looked glamorous), I took a swim myself in the calm waters at the side of the great swirling Zambezi. I may have been in the water for half an hour. It was not until I returned to Lusaka that it was pointed out to me that it was up these quiet side waters that crocodile who might be intent on a spot of fishing themselves might be found. Looking back, I cannot imagine why the risk of proving to be a crocodile's lunch did not occur to me at the time – it might have been my protected upbringing. Nor was that all. For I could have contracted bilharzia, an appalling disease which is prevalent in all African water and is a massive curse throughout the continent. You can get rid of it by spending a few weeks' in London's Hospital for Tropical Diseases. But the vast majority of Africans cannot get there and, in any event, I am told that every day in that institution you get brown soup, which puts one off hospitalisation for life. Further, I doubt if the Burgundy is up to much either.

In my early teens, my parents found an isolated cottage on the Morvern peninsula in Argyll. My brother and I used to disappear up into the hills behind the cottage – this was a good three to four miles uphill. I would not have gone along with this masochism but for the fact that years previously the owners of the estate had stocked the clear clean lochs hidden up there with brown trout. For some reason, nobody from the estate tried to fish there. It must just have been too far and hardly the real thing in comparison to the sea trout and salmon fishing already available. The result was that my brother and I hooked truly colossal catches – I think we might have come home with as many as thirty or more trout on one occasion. Given that the average weight was over half a pound, the task of cleaning the lot on return was quite considerable. I do not think that any member of my family complained. The mood was one of celebration of so great a harvest.

Thirty years on, my family has stayed from time to time at the estate's grand house, Ardtornish, which is owned by the Raven family – I think granny Raven inherited a ton of dough through her family establishing Hay's Wharf. Ardtornish itself is a magnificent late Victorian mansion but impossible to maintain economically today. It must be quite a burden.

I have never been musical or a thespian and, although appreciating painting, I do not do it myself. However, I love word games such as the crossword. I have spent a disproportionate time on them since I am not particularly good at solving them – although I console myself with remarking that, if I were any good (i.e. capable of knocking them off nine times out of ten in five minutes), I would rapidly cease to bother to try.

I suppose the word business just runs in my family. Noam Chomsky has written that one is born with words in one's head and that one merely releases them over time (or something like that). That said, I have never got round to a frequent use of eschscholtzia or floccinaucinihilipilification (Noam has not explained how these two got in on my being conceived). I expect they will be taken up by our cleaner as names for her next two racehorses. I think I should warn her now that, of these two exceptional ideas, the second will be turned down by The Jockey Club since it exceeds eighteen letters. Spoilsports.

I have of course read many crossword clues where I have failed to begin to solve them and have therefore left the allotted space on the crossword empty. I may therefore have missed the best ever clue. That said, I claim that title for: A poor fielder (3,7,7). The answer to this is The Ancient Mariner because he "stoppeth one in three". If it were argued that this clue is a rather recherché snobbery, based as it is on a presumption of knowledge and recall of poetry along with cricket, I would merely mention that I would never have got the answer. It has just been pointed out to me as one of those little jokes that ease the passing of the day.

I quite enjoy a trip to Paris since, after orally fumbling through reception at The Travellers' or wherever, feel sufficiently ashamed to ask my wife – she is a linguist - just how to ask a sensible question of a Parisian. And then, a day or two later, I have felt enough sentences on advertising posters filtering in during my forays to the Agence de Presse that I begin to analyse the text and wish I knew more. Although this attitude runs in the family, I do not take it that seriously, since at that moment of initiation to being a proper Parisian, it is usually time to catch the boat train back to Blighty.

I read of people who were brought up without a single book in their home. I suppose that condition is commoner than is generally recorded – especially nowadays when the time that might have been spent reading is turned to computer games and Sky. However, my childhood was massively book-centred. My parents had (and still have) thousands of books. Some are works of classical scholarship whilst others are philosophical tracts. In short, not the sort of stuff to grab the imagination of a boy. But there was (and is) a huge range of just about everything else under the literary sun. It is worth staying with them for several weeks at a time.

If I were a free man today, I would wander from bookshop to second hand bookshop picking up half a dozen books a day. God knows where I would put them. I just like buying them and securing the hint of fascinating moments to come, which, of course, I never enjoy since nobody can read half a dozen books in a day. Mercifully, I have forgotten my password at www.amazon.com and cannot order from that source. If I were able to, my wife and I might just as well evacuate our home right now. This frequent obsession is well recorded in Anne Fadiman's delightful book, *Ex Libris*.

Bennett Cerf's *Laughing Stock* was the first book that I ever bought with my own money. I was thirteen years old. It was just a paperback joke book and cost two shillings and sixpence. That was one twenty-fourth of my entire term's pocket money. I have always valued jokes very highly and much appreciate today's Internet environment where there is an infinite supply of jokes for no charge. I still have Bennett Cerf.

I have seen this problem of space for books partially conquered by putting bookshelves up the side of one's stairs. This display is quite a good means of reminding oneself what one has got in stock as one trips down to breakfast. Further, if it really gets too much, one can always give them away – for instance my brother and I were beneficiaries of such donations from the collection of the chaplain of University College, Oxford, the Reverend Tom Parker. The remarkable feature of these books was that I think Tom Parker had not read them at all. He had just harvested them in the manner to which I have earlier alluded. The other point about Tom Parker was that you could always tell what he had had for breakfast that morning since the traces were always on his waistcoat – fried eggs featured extensively in his life.

Another way to get rid of books is to lend them, which comes to giving them. This was formally noted by Lord Chesterfield who remarked that he never lent books since they were never returned. He added, "if you doubt that proposition, come along to my library and you will see a lot of books lent to me by a host of bloody fools." I do not know why this behaviour occurs, still less why it is tolerated. I suppose it must be that lending someone a book is slightly personally intrusive so that, if it is not returned, the borrower has accepted oneself, a rather pleasant thought. This may prove that all municipal libraries are agreeable – millions of books are stolen from them each year.

My career at Rugby was wholly undistinguished. However, as did many of my contemporaries, I became interested in politics and the strength of the economy – or the gateway to greater prosperity for all in society. From there it was a relatively short step to wondering just what went on at the London Stock Exchange and why share prices went up and down so much when – at least as far as I could see – life changed so little. This puzzlement was a product of the protected nature of my upbringing.

That was not the only puzzle. Given that I have spent my working life accounting for and monitoring profit, it might be supposed that I was brought up to understand and measure money. I most certainly was not. For instance, when sent shopping by my mother, I just took it for granted that the butcher, the baker and, for all I can recall, the candlestick maker were there simply to serve society. The idea that they specialised the better to serve their customers from whom they sought profit never even remotely crossed my mind. Rent – not that I had the slightest idea of how much rent was paid in what circumstances – was merely a contribution to the expenses of running a property. That rent was determined by supply and demand did not occur to me. And, really, that is not entirely surprising given that my parents never discussed the getting of money.

I failed Cambridge entrance and, since Oxford was out of the question – it being sensibly recognised that a break away from that city would be a sound move, I found myself in early 1965 as an articled clerk with Cooper Brothers and Co, an extremely successful and aggressively run firm of chartered accountants (this firm was one of the antecedents of PriceWaterhouseCoopers today). This was a taste of something different. And from time to time I found it extremely exciting. But I could not begin fully to participate in this excitement since I was so ignorant of just about everything and, most significantly of all, I was unable to write even the simplest business or accountancy-related English. I was therefore excluded from any hope of promotion or personal development in that firm.

Since I did not understand that this was so, I found it very frustrating. Indeed, I was not to improve my ability to communicate in writing until several years later when hunger demanded hard work and the hard work demanded persuading people who were thoroughly awkward. I am drawn to the proposition that few circumstances teach a fellow better than the compulsion to support his family.

I was articled to J Francis Shearer, alas now long since dead. I was in awe of him. He had a particularly striking and handsome appearance and must count as the most patrician chartered accountant that I have ever met.

He was always immensely busy and (a mistake, I think) could only see his articled clerks twice a year – I think that that was a minimum requirement of the Institute.

Mindful that he did not tolerate people who were late, I made a point of being very early for any of these biannual appointments, waiting round the corner from his office for nine o'clock, the appointed hour, struck by the bells of St Paul's which was close by. I would then knock on his door only to be told on most of these occasions that he was busy and that I should come back in half an hour. I did not mind since I was being paid.

The interviews were very short and always based on one question: "Are you so bored with accountancy that you want to pack it in? If so, come and see me." Well, I was not, said so and never took up his offer.

As it happens, I am not an auditor by nature. I am not inherently suspicious of people and I rather pity those who are. And the bulk of my work at Coopers was spent auditing. As it happens, I worked quite hard but was not suited to the work in hand. I never recognised any frauds even though, unwittingly, I may have encountered one.

Nonetheless, I am numerate by birth and qualified as a chartered accountant in 1969 (my next door neighbour in the final examination hall had started taking the exams before the 1948 Companies Act – there's persistence for you) and found myself on a one way ticket to Zambia as an audit senior with Coopers in their Lusaka office. I should add that I had taken the precaution of proposing a few weeks' earlier to my wife to be. She followed on a month or so later and we were married in Leopard's Hill just outside Lusaka. We have two daughters, Lucy (born in 1972) and Emma (born in 1976). Lucy has established Osborne Cawkwell, a tutorial agency, and Emma is turning her hand to graphic design.

Zambia was an education in itself. Before I went there, I believed that the Smith regime (it was always a regime in the British press) was morally wrong and that Britain should forcefully overthrow the Rhodesian Front in order to install black African majority rule. But a few months in Lusaka taught me the total folly of that belief. Further, nothing in the ensuing thirty-two years has caused me to change my mind. To me, it is quite incredible that, in former British colonial territories in Africa, African wages are typically now lower than they were at independence. It is an amazing indictment of the incompetence and corruption of African governments.

Of course, there are many extraordinarily intelligent, brave and principled Africans who know that their countries are ruled by arbitrary and greedy tyrants. But I am afraid that there are just not enough of the good men to go round. And so the cycle of deprivation goes on and on.

Well, by 1973, I could see that there could be no future for my family were we to stay in Zambia. Besides, immigration officials were quite as difficult as any encountered elsewhere in the world. So I doubt if we even had the option to stay. Accordingly, we found ourselves back in London and my needing to find a job. This was not easy given that I had been out of the mainstream of European professional development for four years.

However, I tasted stockbroking (it was only a taste since the total commission earned in five weeks was something of the order of £6) and then got a job as accountant of a commodity actuals firm in Fenchurch Street EC3, Alfred Isaacs and Co. Ltd. This was to be an introduction to things to come in that it was the point at which I started to understand in a practical sense the nature of commerce and the people who work in it. I have always ever since sought to analyse the detail of a business and what each individual does in it. For unless one achieves a proper understanding it is quite impossible to advise on what are usually people problems.

That said, I was not a success at Isaacs – with the benefit of hindsight, the directors (not the Isaacs family) were very foolish and so in May 1975 I organised my temporary book-keeping engagements as Cawkwells, Chartered Accountants. It may seem a laugh now but to me and my wife it was very serious stuff. I followed up newspaper advertisements for assignments in and around north London and gradually the business built up. It was extremely hard and personally rewarding work. It really taught me the nuts and bolts of business. I worked 60 hours and more a week at £2.50 an hour and I look back on that time as the centrally formative years of my life. Many years later I was assisting Ken Dodd when he was accused of criminal evasion of tax. He explained his early career to me by pointing out that he had found an ability to make people laugh and that he had thus been "kissed by an angel". A little later, he asked me about my fees. I said I had started at £2.50 an hour but that I also had been kissed by an angel. He paid up.

I would also mention that there are currently two clients on the books of our small firm that have been there since 1975. This may be through loyalty or it could be through satisfaction. I like to think it is the latter.

In 1976, I answered an advertisement in the *Hampstead and Highgate Express* inserted by a Jack Bennett. He had a myriad of companies all with roughly the same name. The idea was to fob off creditors by denying that any contract with the company identified by the creditor as a debtor was enforceable. His books were an appalling mess because they never came to a conclusion. There was hardly any trade. Loans were received and replaced by further loans. The money was spent inter alia on a chocolate brown Rolls Royce, which he drove down to the Dorchester to interview the targets he intended to deceive. I made my excuses and left.

But he had told me that he had been in a concentration camp in the war. I sympathised with him. The tears seemed genuine enough to me – and with good reason. Whether my sympathy cut any ice or not I cannot now tell (he later did time for a massive fraud and is now dead). However, he introduced me to another survivor of the camps, who at the age of seventeen had made his way to Britain in 1945 – Hitler had murdered the rest of the survivor's family. This businessman had established quite a business wholesaling suitcases, school satchels, fashion bags and so forth. The Revenue wanted his tax affairs brought up to date. When they called on him, he told them to close his account with them. I thought this was a spirited response. Actually, given his time at the hands of the Germans, I expect he reckoned that the Revenue could do little to hurt him.

The job of sorting out his affairs was very extended and, in the end, I sent in a document of fifty pages explaining the assumptions that I had employed to support the figures that I had submitted. The Revenue found it so complex that they nodded through all the accounts and, mirabile dictu, the taxpayer got a refund rather than a demand for tax. He settled my fee account of £3,000 for about two hundred hours' work without a murmur. I think it was my first serious fee. Some readers may wonder whether the refund can have been correct. But it was since the taxation system had gone completely barmy and allowed for tax relief merely through an increase in stock – a figure that is unrelated to profit. The tax system has now ceased to be merely barmy; it is now virtually incomprehensible – this will lead to a crisis in direct taxation.

I also acted for the grandfather of discotheque lighting (or so the trade press described him) and at his instigation accompanied him to Atlantic City in April 1978 to consider the financing and management of the world's first laser discotheque – to be situated at the end of one of the piers. For Atlantic City was on the verge of opening for legalised gambling and nobody knew what the target market of about 90m people within driving distance of Atlantic City would make of it. However, the appeal seemed likely to prove immense and discotheque dancing had acquired a new lease of life through John Travolta in Saturday Night Fever. The project looked to be a runner.

What seemed certain to me as we walked out along the pier with only six weeks to go to the 4th of July, the day when Atlantic City was due to open up in its new phase, was that this pier needed a lot of money spent on it very quickly. For a significant number of boards were missing and the discotheque itself had raw concrete as a dancing floor; we were dealing with the mob and we had USD 72,000 in forged travellers' cheques thoughtfully provided by the venture's Swiss partner who had omitted to come with us at the last minute. The outlook was not propitious.

However, that night, the mob's lawyer picked us up in his Lincoln Continental, which slunk off to dinner at Latz's Knife and Fork Inn. This joint was established in 1904 and presumably so named because at other restaurants people merely used their hands. I got on with this lawyer and he asked me to compere the diving horse which would also be entertaining visitors to the pier later that year. The original horse came up from Florida in the thirties and it and its successors would go up to the top of a rickety diving board fifty feet above a pool and then jump into it with the rider aboard. The trick for the compere was to make the build up last forty minutes before the next lot of paying customers would make their way into the area.

I was offered a thousand dollars a week and expenses for about ten weeks. I turned it down since I had commitments in the UK. Besides, I thought he was kidding. Apparently he was not. I sometimes regret my decision. I am sure I could have done a fortnight. It would have been a paid holiday. Needless to add, the discotheque never proceeded.

I think it is generally accepted that if one acts for an individual, even when that individual has ceased to be a client of one's firm, one is obliged to keep one's personal opinions of that client to oneself. But in describing my relationship with Simon Anthony Fussell, I claim a public interest defence.

In 1980, I put a small advertisement in the Financial Times to the effect that that year's Finance Act had transformed the outlook for venture capital investing and that I saw an opportunity to promote such investments. The programme was to find the opportunities, the entrepreneurs and the managers. There were a number of replies – mostly from crackpots. But one respondent was Simon.

He impressed me enormously. Apart from the fact that he was cheerful, he bubbled with enthusiasm and ideas. He had immense charm. And, as one does, I found myself drawing him into not merely my personal life but also my family's life. I think anybody else would have done exactly the same.

A year or two later, he identified a tiny fully listed shell, Priest Marians PLC, which had, as its sole asset, some development land in Hildenborough, in Kent. The break up value of Marians was about £500,000 and the shares – all 190,000 of them - stood at £2 – in short at an attractive discount. PM was controlled by a former Warburgs dealer and, clearly, Simon charmed him as well into letting Simon have some stock at option and some for cash – but not, of course, control. Simon set about finding deals.

A month or two later, I said to Simon, who had just purchased further PM stock – albeit at a higher price and where he had still not achieved control – that he might be being led up the garden path in that any deal he might offer to PM would be turned down and that, in due course, he would have to sell his stock back to the only person in a position to do anything with it – the dealer who had originally sold. The proceeds would of course be less than that sum originally laid out. Simon was thunderstruck. He might not have thought that my warning as to the outcome was possible or he might have objected to my questioning his judgement. I shall never know.

However, he pushed on and a great credit boom (a period when people increasingly tend to suspend disbelief) gathered pace from 1982 to 1989. Simon took control of PM by injecting properties for stock and declared it an investment company specialising in quality office investment properties in the West End of London. He knows about the design of properties and something of the rental market. He is a bruising negotiator with infinite skill in twisting and turning to his advantage. So, with a mixture of gearing and a rising market, the stock flew. With convinced cheerleaders such as myself in attendance it was positively *de rigueur* to own PM stock.

By 1985, Simon transferred his tax affairs to my office and we set about resolving them. But the staff did not get on with him and, since his principal purpose – as I now recognise it - in contacting my office was to influence me, he did not get on with the staff. The result was that, in February 1988, he withdrew his affairs in favour of Clark Whitehill. In due course, this proved lucky for me. However, because I enjoyed Simon's company, I continued to see him weekly – goodness knows how much we spent at Wiltons, which was directly beneath my then office in Jermyn Street. Although the Savoy Grill may be known as the Deal-Makers' Arms, I submit that the largest deals may well be handled more discreetly at Wiltons.

By 1987, he had also taken control of a small furniture company, Minty PLC, based, as it happens, in Oxford. Again, the stock flew. The concert party – this included my wife as to an investment of the order of £25,000 – saw the stock double, treble and then quadruple on the expectation of a dynamic new force in furniture design emerging. This development seemed plausible to me since Simon knows and cares about the design of furniture – indeed, he had formally studied the design of furniture when he left school.

Much to my surprise, Minty then proceeded to deal in properties, some of which were owned by Simon and others by PM. I could not understand why. After all, why should profit be achieved by the purchaser when it had not so been by the vendor in such circumstances? Further, the furniture business did not prosper – perhaps the shares had been way down for a good reason when Simon had first entered. I did not ask about the property deals since they were nothing to do with me professionally and, besides, taking a close interest in the property deals of a client (former or otherwise) can engender mistrust on the part of the client.

In or about mid 1988, PM's finance director, a sound fellow with a good record, stopped me in Jermyn Street and commented on the acquisition by PM of Local London Group PLC for £110m cash with the assistance of a loan for that sum (i.e. 100% of the consideration) arranged by James Capel. Apparently, Simon had authorised this transaction without any reference to PM's board of directors. I thought this strikingly odd. Further, when I saw Simon a day or two later, he outlined LLG's balance sheet. I was struck that if net asset value was computed after allowing for corporation tax on unrealised gains within LLG's property portfolio, there was a substantial gap below £110m. Simon pointed out that he was confident that values would continue to rise and, because achieved with 100% gearing, enable a new and much higher value for PM's stock. That would allow PM to bid for Great Portland Estates PLC, a very substantial property company some of whose properties were contiguous to those of PM. However, when Simon intimated that he was really set on not merely this merger but on using the yet further enlarged PM for a bid for Land Securities PLC, I decided that he had lost touch with reality. (It should be understood that Land Securities PLC was then, as it is now, Britain's largest property company – and by some margin.) But I did not suspect fraud.

In 1989, with commercial property values increasingly suspect, Simon introduced me to a director of Norton Group PLC, a smallish engineering company born from the old Norton motorcycle company. If matters had hitherto seemed strange to me, they rapidly became surreal. Minty and Norton merged. However, much though Minty's share price kept sagging, I still did not think anything improper had occurred. I think you can now see why I have generally regarded myself as a poor auditor – even if recent years have seen me as quite an effective bloodhound – a different engagement in that a bloodhound is convinced of skullduggery whereas an auditor has to remain constantly aware of its possibility.

Eventually Norton collapsed and inspectors were appointed by the DTI in January 1991 to investigate it. I still did not suspect that Simon would be investigated – although I was mildly surprised to receive an approach from the inspectors in relation to an investment company, Pecos, controlled through an offshore trust associated with Simon. I could not help them.

DTI inspectors' reports are variable in quality but the Norton report, which emerged in 1993, was brilliantly constructed and witty into the bargain. It was only at this point that the scales fell from my eyes. A few months later, Simon was sentenced to two years' imprisonment for fraud. The report reveals the breath-taking extent of it in relation to a number of companies. But I am bound to reflect that it must have extended over many other companies and people not covered in the report.

I occasionally toyed with the proposition that Simon was corrupted by the success of his commercial campaign, which emerged on the stock market from about 1985 onwards. But that seems a foolish idea to me. He seems to me to be a psychopath since, when I described his conduct to a police psychiatrist whom I know well, the psychiatrist so diagnosed and added: "Of course, he was very clever. All psychopaths are." Since psychopaths emerge that way in early childhood it is quite impossible that Simon was turned in 1985. Looking back, he regarded each time he spoke not as an opportunity but as an obligation to mislead. Thus, throughout the time that I knew him, I was being generally had for a fool. I was diminished. I mention all this as a warning to others: one should not tolerate lies or inconsistency of this nature. It ends in tears. Looking back, there was one amusing moment in this sorry tale. In or about 1991 Simon turned to me and remarked that there is no such thing as truth. He failed to see the difficulty that he had set himself by that very statement.

The accountancy business has changed out of all recognition since 1975. During the eighties I noted Lord Benson, formerly senior partner of Coopers and Lybrand, remark that the golden age of accountancy was upon us. He was right. The trouble is that to lock into the profits thereby arising one has had to specialise – particularly in regulated industries. And my firm has always been too small to adapt to the essential economies of scale that regulation demands.

Since I needed the money and had only the haziest idea of my professional liability in the early days of my practice, I took on anything I could. That noted, my small practice generally only considered smallish sums of money in the main and was therefore relatively immune from indemnity litigation. Besides such litigation was then only a trickle by comparison to the torrent that exists today.

One of the assignments undertaken as a result of my policy of doing anything for a crust was an investigation of a shoe factory in Costa Rica in 1982. It came about through my being ushered into the presence of a charming elegant and handsome earl in his extensive Lowndes Square home. He was about twenty-five years old and his personal income was, I was told, then about £1m a month. He wanted to make this investment (costing merely a few months' income) and I was to report upon the business.

A day or two later I flew to Miami with two Italians who owned the shoe factory and who were immaculately mannered and spoke fairly good English. (I, of course, spoke neither Italian nor Spanish.) At Miami, we were due to take a further flight on to San Jose, Costa Rica's capital. We were just about to board when one of the Italians was held back by immigration control. So we sat around for a further six hours until he re-emerged rather irritably pointing out that they had got the wrong man.

At San Jose, we were met by a medium-sized but strongly built chauffeur at the wheel of a Mercedes 600. He had once been personal bodyguard to the president of Nicaragua, a General Somoza, who had needed a bodyguard if anybody ever did – he was assassinated in Paraguay in 1980. The chauffeur had a flashing smile and was now employed by the Italians.

The Mercedes swept towards central San Jose in a Graham Greene setting of decrepit lorries overloaded down to the axles. It thrust up a hill and at the click of a control switch the vast gates of a giant hacienda swung open to admit the weary travellers. Several servants emerged to handle our baggage and we were led up to a magnificent drawing-room with glass sides all round looking out over San Jose.

I was introduced to the Secretary of the National Assembly. He was modest and unassuming and I presumed that he was the equivalent of our clerk to the House of Commons. He was actually the equivalent of prime minister. He explained that there was no corruption in Costa Rica. This may be so but I was at a loss to explain how a man who was self-confessedly paid $20,000 p.a. could afford to live in such style. I can of course guess.

After a superb dinner, I crawled exhausted into bed at about 2.30 a.m. local time. One of the Italians and the ever-attentive chauffeur made off into San Jose to sample some nightlife. However I was determined to hit the ground running and had agreed to visit the first factory at 7.30 a.m. So you can imagine my surprise when the chauffeur was on hand at that time the following day seemingly fresh and certainly uncomplaining even though I doubt if he had had any sleep to speak of. He buckled on his shoulder holster. This struck me as slightly concerning since I had not realised before going that armed robbery was and I presume remains all the rage in Central America. On more than one occasion lying awake in bed in the middle of the night as the assignment unfolded I heard shots – and they were not that far away. So either Costa Ricans just fancy nocturnal target practice or burgling is a pretty risky business in the territory.

My assignment had started simply on the assumption that I would review the books of account and extrapolate using common sense. But I was able to strengthen my presentation greatly by recruiting a study mate from my time at Rugby, Christopher Pitt. He specialised in shoe–making machinery and associated materials and flew in from the United States a day later. His father had been in the Royal Navy, as had the Earl's solicitor, Commander Lennox Cotton, who had also arrived. The naval men liaised well. Lennox Cotton was a really remarkable man from whom I learnt much including the advice that one should write down as little as possible. I have never followed this advice – I rather practise the reverse – and this perversity on my part has now cost me a lot of money.

Costa Rica then owed something like $2bn in debt. There was no chance of it repaying more than a tiny fraction because there are only 2m citizens and average monthly wages were of the order of $30. How this debt was contracted I cannot begin to imagine.

But the effect was that Costa Rica enjoyed preferential export opportunities to the US, which was then very concerned to see that communism did not spread through Central America. The US was determined to sponsor local employment and industry. The shoes produced could therefore be theoretically sold at around $6 a pair into the southern states of the US. Further, Costa Rican legislation insisted that all cow hides had to be offered for sale firstly to the shoe factory. So I took the view that all essential supplies of materials and labour and the company's markets were secure. Further, Christopher advised that the machinery was modern and in good working order.

However, from here matters tended to unravel. The business was heavily in debt and the machinery seemed very expensive in relation to the figures that Christopher had expected. This was not surprising because the machinery had first been sold to associates of the P2 Masonic lodge in Italy and uplifted by about 100% profit before Italian governmental overseas aid finance derived through Banco Ambrosiano saw the machinery installed in Costa Rica. It has been my unvarying experience that corrupt businessmen are also bad managers of a business: they always take their eye off the ball.

Finally, as we left Costa Rica, the management thrust six pairs of shoes into my and Christopher's hands as parting gifts. This was a mistake since Christopher's laboratory subsequently analysed them and determined that the shoes would last ten days at most and then, only as long as conditions were dry. It is utterly astonishing to me that this sort of aid finance is ever extended by anybody.

I see a photograph of the earl from time to time in a Dempster diary story - usually based round his latest marriage. The Italian who was detained at Miami airport was declared a wanted man over Costa Rican radio a few months later – he was reportedly associated with the Red Brigades in Italy. With the Airports blocked, I think he got out over the border into Nicaragua. I doubt if he is in the shoe business these days. And I got a £4,000 fee for ten days' work. That's accountancy for you.

Politically, I have moved from mildly left wing to libertarian right. It has not been difficult to do. Harold Wilson (PM 1964 to 1970 and 1974 to 1976) may have had the common touch. But, quite unquestionably, he was common. I think it was said that his was the best first class degree in economics awarded at Oxford between the first and second world wars – though quite how such comparisons are made is not obvious to me. But at the practical level of handling the economy he always took the soft option – this meant appeasing the trades unions so that the country was permanently ground to a standstill at the whim of some blockhead in Birmingham. Marginal taxation rates ensured that no sane fellow would enter industry. Or, if he would, not in the UK.

Sterling was overvalued because markets were not allowed to dictate its rate. (I always thought the move to a floating rate of exchange in the late sixties was obviously sensible. Given the then Labour government's experience, just how the Conservatives should have made the same mistake in the early nineties is beyond me.) The result was permanent impoverishment of the entire country. So I departed from the Labour Party's ranks of sympathisers.

Looking back, Heath was also a disaster while Callaghan, although he knew that his party was stupid, did practically nothing to bring it to heel. For instance, I still wonder at how marginal income taxation rates of 83% and more were regarded as sensible – Dennis Healey was indeed a very silly billy. I am certain that any claim that he did not believe in this approach to taxation but merely tolerated it to appease his party's lunatic left is wrong. In the early eighties, I met Sir Leo Pliatzky who had been permanent secretary at HM Treasury during Healey's years and he told me that Healey really believed his own silly ideas.

It was not until Thatcher took over in 1979 that I had any sense of wise and effective government. However, strangely, by 1985/86, I had the feeling that the Conservatives were losing a grip on basic libertarian principles and reverting to the usual meddling state that is Britain. This feeling persists; it depresses me.

I think I am contrary by nature. This tendency was spotted fairly early on by my father who recounted to me the story concerning the late Professor Sir Ronald Syme who, at a meeting of Oxford's Congregation (its parliament), noted that the bulk of dons were taking a particular stance and remarked that, since they could not all be right, they had to be wrong and that he would therefore vote for the other side. There is a temptation to be mischievously perverse where debate cannot reasonably be promoted. I am frequently tempted. (Whether stock market bears are mischievously perverse or not they certainly lead lonely lives and, when joined by others, are in greatest danger because ideal trading conditions for bears occur when the vast majority are buying on the other side.)

The sport that has obsessed me since I was sixteen has been horseracing and betting thereon. I was introduced to it by Peter Cundell, whose study was opposite mine at Rugby. His father, Ken, had had a runner in the 1963 Oaks, Pourparler, ridden by Scobie Breasley and Peter told me to back it each way at 14/1. Which I did – I think I had four shillings each way. It came second and I was hooked.

In those days, the Times racing correspondent, perhaps ten times a year, not merely selected a horse for a race but described it as a "confident selection". This was pointed out to me by a Rugbeian contemporary's father, who worked at Alexander's Discount House. I think he had eschewed the affiliated company, which had a ragtime band. The confident selection worked a treat throughout the rest of the sixties. Indeed, I relied upon it. Who would not have? The Times has stopped this practice now. I do not know why. But I suppose it is nearly impossible to pick up valuable information as a racing correspondent to share with readers without destroying the price.

The racecourse market was my introduction to markets in general. Looking back, I suppose that I would have simultaneously learnt about stock markets had I had any money to invest – which, of course, I had not. So that pleasure took some years to come to fruition.

But I was aware of the stock market – after all, I read the Financial Times assiduously every day. Since I was a very callow young man I did not understand the bulk of what I read. All I can say now is that I took it very seriously. I reckoned that, if one were to go on studying, the penny would eventually drop. This has proved to be true.

I think I should mention that gambling has also caused me immense troubles in that debt has more than once threatened to consume me. On the other hand, it has had its amusing side. For instance, in 1989, when it was long odds against my settling the Winter term's fees for my elder daughter at Rugby, I was rescued by placing £3,000 to win £40,000 on Secretary Of State in a big handicap at Newmarket. To my intense relief, it scooted home by five lengths thus enabling me to write to the bursar of Rugby "…I enclose my cheque as a result of the surprising and active intervention of the relevant secretary of state….".

Another influence in my development was an awareness at the time of its emergence as a force in the land, of Slater Walker Securities. Run by Jim Slater from the mid sixties to the mid seventies, it seemed to be practically everywhere all at the same time. He realised that British industry and commerce was hopelessly badly run and that a minor push or two would release the hidden assets. He gave more than one or two minor pushes. Apparently, every year, tens of former staff of SWS still assemble for a reunion. That is quite a thought given that SWS itself went belly up in 1975.

Looking back, it is clear to me that Britain was class ridden and just asking to be broken up. Jim took fairly ordinary fellows from fairly ordinary backgrounds and persuaded them that they could challenge the established financial institutions. They did. Although history must record that some of the SWS operatives were spivs (or worse) and that their operations were questionable, there can be no doubt that SWS played a prominent part in changing corporate Britain. For it became obvious to all young men (and, eventually, young women) that it was not necessary to have a family background connected to the City to enter that stimulating arena and cop a fortune. And the fact is that Britain has emerged some twenty-five years later as the premier financial centre in the world barring New York – and there is no guarantee that New York's supremacy is unassailable. Perhaps London would have got here in any event. But I rather think that SWS and its founder played a considerable if unintended role.

I was introduced to Jim in March 1993. I was struck by his unassuming approach. He related how he had been invited to spend Christmas 1992 as a guest of Sir James Goldsmith in his splendid Mexico property. He had declined. I sympathised, remarking that leaving the market for ten days could be very expensive. He immediately countered that that was not his consideration. He was concerned that from day one of his stay he would be orally assaulted by Sir James, a forceful fellow if ever there was one, over breakfast compelling him to sell out (Sir James was a serious bear) such that, eventually, he would do just that when, in his heart of hearts, he was immensely bullish – he had realised the latent force that was the gathering lunacy of the US mutual fund industry. For my part, I noted his tendency to listen to the other side. (For the record, had I been the guest in Mexico, I would not have changed my mind at all – I was almost as bearish as Sir James. I also mention that Sir James took being bearish very seriously. I know this because I met his index-trading dealer a few months after Sir James's death in 1997. He assured me that, in or about 1991, Sir James had blown upwards of £30m on the bear tack.)

Some will yawn at my frequent carping at regulators. They may well be right. Certainly I remember a junior member of a MacMillan cabinet who had picked up a knighthood and subsequently wrote as Jack Logan in *The Sporting Life*. Here, he constantly, week in, week out, criticised The Jockey Club. As a result, a lot of people thought he was just a bore at one level and silly at another. Perhaps I have run the same risk. But I still think that time will show that a lot of regulation as practised in and around the stock market is very expensive and achieves remarkably little. Further, the arrogance of the regulators is breath-taking. And I object to that whether they are doing a good job or not.

Finally, my friend, Nigel Johnson-Hill, says that, as a matter of principle, I am against regulation. He is right. Worse, the climate will continue to deteriorate in this regard from now until my death. It is all very dreary.

THE ART OF SHORTING

"As for the virtuous poor, one can pity them, of course but one cannot possibly admire them."
- Oscar Wilde, the Soul of Man Under Socialism.

My first book, Profit Of The Plunge (*POTP*), was published in 1995 and covered short-selling. It was the first book in the UK so to do. It has enjoyed a mild success but not that great a success. It is now out print. But Tom Winnifrith of t1ps.com thought that a further book might assist – partly to update *POTP* but also to include my views on buying equities for the long term. Given that I am widely believed only to short stocks this book is an opportunity for me to correct this misunderstanding.

Several readers will note that I have reproduced extensively from *POTP*. I do not apologise for having so done – after all, both *POTP* and this book are primarily intended as books to assist investors with the nuts and bolts of short-selling. But, equally, I have cut out much of the merely illustrative parts of *POTP* in the belief that events have taken over and fresh illustrations have become available. However, I make not even a hint of an apology for including my engagement with Maxwell since the DTI report into the activities surrounding the flotation of Mirror Group has now been published – in early 2001 or more than eleven years after the frauds were committed. I have read this report and it changes nothing that I originally wrote. I would only add that the tone of the report is very much determined with the benefit of hindsight. Many think that that is not available in real life.

What is a Short?

Short-selling (or going a "bear") is the process of selling stock which one does not own in the expectation of buying it back later at a lower price and thus realising a profit. Because there must always be the possibility that no stock is available when one comes to buy to close the short-sold position, there must always be the theoretical possibility that one can lose all that one has. Indeed, so awful is such a prospect that some otherwise apparently sensible people claim that one can lose an infinite amount of money. But, however much money is in the world, the total is surely finite. So one can dismiss the "infinite" argument against short-selling as the commentary of the cowardly and ignorant - and one always does well by ignoring that lot.

The morality of short-selling

It has often been remarked to me that short-selling is somehow "bad form". Such commentators opine that, in life, if one has nothing positive to say, one should say nothing. It is further argued that short-selling is a negative statement in itself and therefore contrary to society's best interests. But all that a short-seller is doing is reflecting upon his perception of the truth. By the time that a company has entered the short list to be sold, the change in its circumstances has either occurred or is about to occur in any event. It can be argued that rescue finance and/or a rescue order might be deterred by a seemingly artificially depressed price. But that seems a most improbable scenario. Besides, God help the over-confident short-seller that meets the buying orders of a broker for the client who reckons the short-seller has made a mistake about the supposedly beleaguered company.

I would also add that forever talking up the value of assets (which process notably occurred through the agency of the Conservatives and their leader in the mid-1980s, particularly in relation to houses) is much more dangerous: when such bubbles are punctured, the fallout is socially much more serious. The proper conclusion is that accentuating the negative to excess is just as unwise as accentuating the positive to excess. Further, if one buys stock in the normal manner, one is invariably encountering a seller. Is this seller to be pilloried for being negative? Let us not forget that all market-makers are frequently short.

It might be thought that because investment institutions do not generally engage in short-selling there is some reason for this policy based on morality rather than profit. But investment institutions must be careful to avoid offending the managements of potential future investments; so short-selling would not be their natural inclination. Further, such institutions are run by fund managers who are almost invariably proscribed from short-selling on their own account. Were institutions to confront the possibility of their fund managers short-selling through their own broker for their own account but ahead of major disposals by their employers, a major temptation to abuse their clients' interests would have to be faced. It can, of course, be argued that managers own long positions could be handled and thus abused in the same manner. But the temptation thus arising would be much less frequent unless the fund manager's personal portfolio matched his employer's - and, then, if he is honest, he might just as well invest in his employer's fund.

I would mention that there have been a number of instances of rights issues in recent years, which, had investors been better informed, would never have been taken up. One that comes to mind was that by Cedar in 1999 for £60m of convertible loan stock when Cedar's shares stood at around £6. Tim Steer, then of Collins Stewart, wrote an inspired circular entitled TIMBER which ravaged Cedar's accounting practices and which I helped to bring to a wider audience via t1ps.com. Unfortunately, it never received enough of an airing through organised short-selling practice and the rights issue succeeded. It never should have. Cedar shares were around 5p when I last looked. In effect, scarce capital has been blown on a bad project.

I should add that a friend, now 80 years old, had a father who, he says, wrote in the 1930s against short-selling. He has often promised to let me have a copy of this tract. But to date he has not been successful. This may be just as well since the chances of the argument being successfully developed strike me as practically zero.

Unlimited losses?

I noted above that in practice the idea that one can rack up unlimited losses from shorting is tosh. However, one cannot rule out facing technical conditions, which can be extremely expensive to surmount. This is not a game for wimps. I am here reminded of the bear "squeeze" which arose in Acorn Computers about fifteen years ago at a time when that company was experiencing commercial difficulty. Although short-sellers were entirely correct to expect declines of the order of 50%+ from the points at which they sold, there was not that much stock about or to be offered by later sellers. As a result, the market-makers (all of whom were perfectly well aware that Acorn Computers was standing at too high a price) simply declined to offer short-sellers stock to enable them to satisfy their short-sale bargains. This was the making of a classic bear squeeze. Before long, one or two short-sellers lost their nerve (this often happens with a short-seller who has not taken the trouble to work out his strategy but, instead, has idly left his decisions to trade to another) and ran for cover. This drove up the price. And only those who had done their homework (and were thus able to resist any argument to justify the new and much higher price) stood their ground.

It has been pointed out to me that the American drinks firm, Snapple, was ludicrously overvalued for a long time and that the shorters held their position confident that they would get justice in the end. In the event, however, Snapple was taken over by Quaker Oats and the shorters were roasted. The fact that the acquisition of Snapple subsequently destroyed Quaker Oats was no comfort at all.

Indeed, as it happens, there have been some famous short squeezes in the US Resorts International, the casinos concern, in the latish seventies which bust a number of short-sellers.

If I were asked to remark upon a general rule as to the potential loss on a short position, I would reply that a dogmatic view is not possible. The fact is that a takeover bid can be at a 100%+ premium to the current price particularly if market conditions are about to turn to the bull tack. The fact is that a highly geared company, even if in its last months of life, can advance quite spectacularly in percentage terms if the market senses that a rescue can be dreamt up. On balance, one should reserve for a loss of the order of 100% of the opening sale proceeds on each position and, on this basis, never commit oneself to an exposure in excess of 10% of one's net wealth. One must always judge whether one's personal balance sheet is excessively geared even though short-sale positions tend to do better when general market conditions are generally bearish.

Some short-sellers of the past: speculative positions; rapid downward price movements caused in the unwinding of speculative positions; who benefited?

(i) Vanderbilt and three corners
A complete history of short-selling would have to encompass the development of stockmarket regulation and much else besides. Obviously, there is insufficient room even remotely to permit such a tedious recital. Further, it would be incomplete in one sense because, as far as I am aware, there are no detailed records of trading on (for instance) the London stockmarket in Victorian times. And I must presume that there are many exchanges around the world whose history has never been closely recorded. For instance, while we are about it, I would not mind betting that the story of Shanghai, to name but one centre, would interest many. The Shanghai story will also remain untold.

Nowadays, one should not, if a director of a company, short-sell the company's stock when a rights issue is on the way. This is because it would be an insider trade. (Mind you, I saw that very conduct several times in the late 1980s.) However, there were no such inhibitions in New York during the nineteenth century. Indeed, it would have been regarded as foolish not to have taken advantage of such an opportunity. That said, one should not be too sanctimonious about Americans: in 1912, Rufus Isaacs, later the first Marquess of Reading, bought American Marconi stock for himself and his Cabinet colleagues ahead of the publication of a contract between the Government and the English Marconi Company. The contract had been negotiated by himself on behalf of the Government. His brother, Godfrey, was a director of English Marconi. Isaacs still became Lord Chief Justice.

There were then many examples of companies controlled from Wall Street by financiers who sold short their companies' stock and then delivered by the simple expedient of selling a "property" (an industrial concern) to their company in exchange for shares. Strictly speaking, this was not short-selling - because the directors knew they would not be going short by the point when delivery would be compelled. But, technically, until the stock had been issued, they would have been short.

This technique of introducing "properties" was a clear opportunity to "water" stock. In nineteenth century markets, there was a lot of "stock watering" - a term derived from the practice of cramming cattle with salt so that the satiation of their resultant thirst pushed up their weight at the point of sale. Many varieties of derring-do were rampant in nineteenth century New York. But, undoubtedly, Vanderbilt's two Harlem corners and his Hudson corner still provoke some admiration for his forthright manner during their development.

The New York and Harlem Railroad joined Wall Street at the southern end of Manhattan to Harlem in the north. It had restricted trading opportunities since it was licensed by the Common Council of New York, the local authority. In early 1863, it occurred to some members of that Council, who presumably owed some duty of fiduciary care to the electors (rather, as I must suppose, did the Marquess of Reading) that it would be a good idea to go long of Harlem stock, grant a franchise to Harlem, and then sell the stock that they had acquired. I am quite sure that it had never occurred to them that this was or would be an undisclosed profit for which, by today's legal standards, they would be obliged to account to the electorate. Further, today, they would be regarded as having breached the obligation of a servant or agent to avoid a conflict of interest. They simply regarded it as a perquisite of election to the Common Council.

Harlem's stock had been standing at $6 in October 1857, attaining $28 by early January 1863. As one of America's financial and commercial titans, Cornelius Vanderbilt took control in the opening months of 1863. The price rose - to $87 by early May 1863. There were 57,000 shares in issue. These figures give some idea of the true forces behind the subsequent movement. I regret that I do not hold indices for either the New York Stock Exchange (NYSE) or railroad stocks in general to allow for adjustment for relative strength. But it is very probable that Harlem had far outperformed the market by early May 1863 notwithstanding the inflationary conditions caused by the Civil War. Harlem may indeed have seemed overbought. The Common Council members schemed first to acquire Harlem stock and then to sell a franchise to Harlem (both of which they did) to extend its operations for 10% of the turnover generated and a flat annual charge of $25 per railcar - a charge, all told, to the franchisee of approximately $300,000 pa. This figure was rated by the market as highly profitable to Harlem. The scheme had the undisclosed distinction of an intention to repeal the franchise after the Common Council members had short-sold the stock.

The combined effect of the Councilmen's initial long positions and Vanderbilt's further purchases caused Harlem to touch $116.25 by 18 May. At this point, the Councilmen clandestinely liquidated their longs through the market to, as it turned out, Vanderbilt and his associates and proceeded to go short. The price declined to $109 by 1 June and $106 four days later. By 9 June it stood at $97.5 and crashed to $83 the following morning, only to recover to $89 that afternoon. However, by 17 June, it stood at $77. And, on 18 June it was traded down to $69.5, even if jumping to $79 in the afternoon.

The Councilmen then decided to cover their shorts. But, being professional men, they did so after announcing that the franchise to Harlem had been rescinded. After all, it helps to see that stock is to hand when one wishes to buy. However, the stock only fell to $72 on the announcement of the rescission. This was because Vanderbilt was supporting the price. It was then that the squeeze started and, two days later, Harlem had risen to $94. By 27 June, it had touched $106. It was then that the Councilmen met and rescinded the rescission subject to their being allowed to close their shorts at $94.

One contemporary writer remarked that: "it may seem anomalous that Harlem should rise 30% on the repeal of the grant and fall on the repeal of the repeal". Many would agree even now. But there was still a short position and, despite civil unrest in New York quite otherwise occasioned,

Harlem showed massive strength throughout July and hit $135 by 4 August and $179 on 24 August. The highest bargain was 500 shares at $180. And that was that. The corner was settled and Vanderbilt let the price drift. By December, Harlem stood at $87.5 -which was probably about where it should have been all along. The approximate decline in value of the company from its high was $5,000,000. This is a helpful sum today. But then, it was astronomic.

Astonishingly, Vanderbilt, who must have had the coolest of cool heads, a sort of cucumber of the century, was simultaneously handling a quite separate operation in Hudson railroad stock. Its price had declined to $123 by 20 June 1863 as a result of a sustained bear-raid. Vanderbilt instructed his brokers to buy all stock that was to hand. He then pulled the masterstroke. He sold his stock and simultaneously bought call options to get it back. This was leaked by Vanderbilt to the short-sellers, who, knowing that such a transaction is very expensive finance in effect, judged that Vanderbilt was short of cash. Accordingly, they sold the stock again through the market to, of course, Vanderbilt, who then exercised his options and called for his stock. The bear-raiders looked round for some. It just was not there and Hudson, on 9 July, hit $180 for cash settlement because Vanderbilt had made it plain that he wanted his stock and would not countenance delay - I presume that any failure to deliver under the then rules of the NYSE would have seen the defaulting short-seller bought-in (q.v.) at market price.

This price contrasted with the simultaneous price for delivery of stock two weeks later of $150. I expect that such quotations were borne in mind by Goldman Sachs when they squeezed the London market in Maxwell Communication Corporation stock some 128 years later.) Vanderbilt then lent stock to the market at 2% per day. Nice business if you can get it. And Vanderbilt got it. Having got it, he forced the bears to close and, that done, the price withered away to $140 a week later. Child's play, really. In 1864, only a year later, Harlem, which was clearly one of those stocks one never holds (because they are only for buying and selling), re-emerged as a scam vehicle. For, despite the New York Councilmen's experience in 1863, some New York State senators, based in Albany, took up long positions and then spread the belief that legislation to assist Harlem's position would be passed. This took the stock up from the low $100s to $149 by mid-March. The senators and their associates closed their longs, opened their short positions and awaited the Senate's judgement. This was indeed that the legislation sought for Harlem would not be passed. And, by 26 March 1864, Harlem had fallen back to $101.

Vanderbilt watched all this and proceeded to build his corner. In fact, he bought so much Harlem stock that his total holding exceeded Harlem's entire issued capital by 27,000 shares. His control of Harlem meant that he knew that there was no chance of more shares being issued. So from its low of $101, Harlem advanced to $122 by 31 March and, by 18 April, to $195. Incidentally, the 18 April sixty day delivery price was $168 - as clear a backwardation pursuant to a bear squeeze as one could ever use by way of illustration. By mid-July, it touched $285. Vanderbilt had played the same stock twice and won.

En passant, I do not think Vanderbilt can have been a very nice man. For it is recorded that, at the outset of the Hudson squeeze, referred to earlier, he had advised his own son to sell 10,000 Hudson shares at $110 -just so that he could get hold of stock. But his son, judging that his father would or might deceive him, bought rather than sold. This made the son a substantial profit. It will be seen that today's legislation covering disclosure of holdings, particularly directors' holdings and concert parties would make Vanderbilt's game much harder to copy. Indeed, it is probably impossible. I qualify impossible" because I reckon that it is wise to assume that anything is possible in a stockmarket.

(ii) Clarence Hatry
When a short-seller is assessing the mood of the market in general while preparing for the big raids, he is obliged to consider the market's participants who are most prominent at the time. Clarence Hatry started his public financial career in the early 1920s. By 1929, aged not quite 40, he had developed a powerful following from the public, which was indifferent to the wisdom of the ventures proposed and assembled by him. It simply felt that his companies were part of the high speed development of the

economy that fortune had dictated as wise and sustainable. Hatry covered all manner of industries: finance companies for stores, automatic vending machines, automatic photography machines and, last but far from least, the rationalisation of the entire iron and steel industry. It is interesting to note that, in principle, if not in execution, these were all sound ideas. But it remains unlikely that any one man could simultaneously co-ordinate the management required to make them succeed.

Hatry's Corporation and General Securities Limited (another example of a name that sounded too important to be taken seriously) had set out in 1925 to arrange municipal loans. It had succeeded. By 1928, Corporation and General Securities Limited's projects were greatly expanded. This required yet more money. But there was only so much appetite for these issues and, as a result, he had to use inter-connected companies and false accounting to make them palatable. There was at least one resignation, by a director who was also a partner in Foster and Braithwaite, the company's brokers - who also resigned at the same time. This was probably an important resignation - Foster and Braithwaite still trade today.

This should have warned the market. It failed to do so because, as an authoritative contemporary record shows, it was accompanied by "plausible reasons". The truth is that when the market wishes to be deceived it is quite unnecessary to take any trouble over the matter. The market has already taken all the trouble that is required to deceive itself. By early 1929, Hatry was desperately short of cash. His municipal loan business was increasingly questioned and he turned to forging stock certificates to offer as collateral. With the money thus raised he forced up Corporation and General Securities Limited's share price and that of each of his other vehicles. The support operation entailed the connivance of a jobber, perhaps sixty brokers on the buying side and a tenth of that number on the selling side. These circumstances must have been noted in the market by short-sellers because brokers tend to be garrulous. And, whereas one or two might be relied upon to be discreet, there is no chance that sixty could be. Short-sellers must have made a fortune.

The bubble burst in September 1929 - the prices of all of Hatry's quoted vehicles halved and more in a day. Dramatically, Hatry asked his chairman, Lord Winchester (who seems to have omitted to take along his rifle), to Room 80 of the Charing Cross Hotel. Hatry, for himself and three associates, said: "We have sent for you to tell you that we are all criminals".

After that, they gave themselves up. No defence solicitor today would countenance such frankness. Equally, no alleged criminal would then have had to face the panoply of absurd laws that we have today. Perhaps the moral climate is unchanged.

It has been absurdly argued that Hatry caused the October 1929 crash on Wall Street. The truth is that stocks were grossly overblown worldwide. To be sure, Hatry had taken advantage of the general climate of self-deception. But the causes of the self-deception were within the hearts of men everywhere and they have been developing since Prehistoric times.

(iii) Wall Street, 1919 to 1932 - Allan Ryan
As considered elsewhere in this book, securities industry regulation has been prompted by excesses leading to damage of the small investor or loss of reputation of the market. The reforms of the handling of capital in America (principally those provided by the Securities and Exchange Commission or SEC) were prompted by the period from 1919 on through the 20s to Wall Street's nadir in 1932. There were many remarkable series of dealings. The first bizarre series that remains popularly recorded was Allan Ryan's squeeze on Stutz, the maker of the Stutz "Bearcat". By early 1920, Stutz itself was considerably reduced but Ryan, who controlled it and was himself a member of the NYSE, squeezed the stock up from $100 to, eventually, $750. The "Business Conduct Committee" of the NYSE charged Ryan with unethical dealing.

Apparently, a number of members of the committee were short themselves. So the committee threatened suspension of the stock from trading - this would make buying to close undelivered short positions according to the exchange's rules much harder. This did not interest Ryan who, although heavily in debt, advised the committee that he would proceed against the exchange to enforce delivery of stock. That caused the NYSE's "Law Committee" to rule that all his purchase bargains were void and that stock would not require to be delivered. The really important point to make here is that if ever one puts market professionals under serious pressure, they will always consider changing the rules to suit themselves. That remains as true today as it was in 1920. Ryan negotiated and supplied stock at $550 per share to short-sellers. Matters were settled. That said, by mid-1922, Ryan was bankrupt with liabilities exceeding assets to the extent of $32m.

(iv) Wall Street, 1919 to 1932 -Clarence Saunders and Piggly Wiggly
Clarence Saunders's Piggly Wiggly was a successful retailing chain of self-service stores, which was bear-raided in mid-1922. The stock was $50. There were 200,000 shares in issue. By early 1923, Saunders had pushed the price up to $70. He was well aware that he would eventually have to reduce his personal indebtedness and that this would entail reducing his holding in Piggly Wiggly. So he offered stock through newspaper advertisements at $55 with the difference that he offered them on deferred terms, which meant that stock would not be released by him and thus made available to short-sellers until the final installment had been paid - this was due nine months after the first $25 payment. Of course, he still possessed about 190,000 shares.

The squeeze started and, by late March 1923, took the price up to $120. The NYSE suspended trading in Piggly Wiggly and, worse, extended the delivery date for short-sellers. This was most unfair to Saunders. Some settlements were achieved with the market at $100. But, as with Stutz, Piggly Wiggly was an unsound company and however much Saunders attempted to manipulate the price the underlying trading position meant any long position was inherently dangerous. Saunders was personally bankrupted in late '23. Saunders reappeared as "The Clarence Saunders, Sole Owner of My Own Name, Stores Inc." This failed in 1930 because of the Great Depression. He died in 1953.

Psychological considerations
Short-selling is usually (but not as its name suggests) a short-term

operation. It is possible, as is considered elsewhere in this book, to borrow stock and remain short for many months - perhaps even years. But the generality of dealing is short-term with constant reviews of short-term decisions. This process, even if intellectually rigorously conducted, attracts gamblers. So a short warning is included. It has to be short because this is a book about short-selling and not psychology, an interesting but entirely different subject.

Some emerge as gamblers from childhood and others do not. I did. But my brother did not. And my sister does not even find the subject interesting. So, simply at my personal family level, I hesitate to be dogmatic as to the cause of the gambling streak. That said, it has been argued in *Encyclopaedia Britannica* (and who am I to argue with such a source?) that gamblers frequently experienced or think that they experienced absolute authority in childhood. I think that this probably fits my own position. And I mention this to force the reader to categorise his or her own position. Failure to do so must cause the gambler to fail because he cannot best judge his position if he is unable to understand his own mental disposition. Failure to understand will always cause losses.

So important is this central control that I urge an investor, if he is in doubt, to take professional advice. A moment's reflection will confirm that £250 spent in Harley Street is rather cheaper than going bust. Besides, going bust is inconvenient.

It might be concluded from the foregoing that I would counsel a gambler altogether to stay away from the market. And I suppose that, in a sense, that conclusion is reasonable. However, provided the gambler understands his disposition, I think he must also recognise that he has one priceless advantage, viz, the vast majority of investors are so concerned at the slightest loss that they find it impossible to trade successfully in the short-term. They make a market for those with a steelier nerve and thus, quite possibly, a better long-term view. Nervous investors cannot make bold decisions and, as a result, they make nothing or lose. They can only watch their capital tend to match long-term trends and opportunities in the markets. Their brains tend to atrophy. And they bore the pants off me.

MARKET MADNESS

"The Best way to get the better of temptation is just to yield to it"
- Clementina Stirling Graham, 1895

In 1995, it seemed to me that we were only months away from a strong setback in world stock markets – indeed, I cashed up all my and my wife's pension fund assets from equities into straight cash – where it has remained ever since. By August 1998, it seemed to me certain that I had called the top three years too early but that I would surely get my view vindicated given the collapse of commercial confidence that then seemed to be spreading from the Far East.

In the event, Alan Greenspan, boss of the US Federal Reserve Bank, reduced interest rates so that investors just had to get out of cash and into equities. We were then struck by an entirely unprecedented mania in the shape of the boom in Internet, Technolgy, Media and Telecoms (TMT) stocks. Nobody had ever seen anything like it.

For me it started – in early 1999 - with losses of £150,000 or so through Internet stock price surges, which had seemed to me to be absolutely impossible. I was bruised – to put it mildly. But I realised that something very curious was going on in that investors were taking collective leave of their senses. We have always met fools in our lives – but it is rare indeed that the market as a whole goes completely mad.

So from mid 1999 onwards I bought stocks, which, in the normal run of things, I would never have considered buying at even a fifth of the prices that I was then paying. I was momentum investing – and in spades. I was not worried since I saw no sign of the lunacy ending. And that is the skill in momentum investing. I got back my £150,000 and a great deal more.

I did not succeed universally – far from it. For instance, I was assured that the Mirror's City Slickers would run a story the following day on the merits of Pacific Media. Knowing the staggering following that that column had generated (incidentally, when they were charged with breaches of the

Press code, they had the immediate defence that the Mirror, particularly their page, was not a newspaper but a comic and that the Press code, which demanded that they should not have invested in companies about which they wrote, therefore did not apply), I looked up Pacific's balance sheet on REFS, the indispensable guide for investors, and saw that there was a £40m capitalisation – at 2.4p – as against net tangible asset value of practically zero. I declined to trade. The following day, the "story" appeared and in volumes of several tens of millions the shares rose to 3.6p. I had therefore missed out on an opportunity to make (say) £24,000 – it would have been a cinch to buy 2m.

But the Slickers were, perhaps accidentally, mining a very deep and rich vein of British silliness and, a day or two later, repeated their original hopes for Pacific such that the stock popped up a further 2p. Finally, their forecast of a deal actually materialised and the stock hit 17.5p. So my original contemplated purchase of 2m shares would have been worth a helpful £300,000 profit at that point.

However, gravity being what it is (it tends to reassert) Pacific Media today sits at around 1.2p. This suggests to me that playing momentum is a dangerous game.

Textbook Madness

Mind you, it was everywhere to be had. A host of wholly improbable stories and companies rocketed up. The TMT boom really took hold. There were so many instances of lunacy that, were one to list and describe each and every one, 1,000 pages at least would be required and one still would not cover all the major examples. But I have chosen Internet Indirect as the *piece de resistance*. It is unquestionably the textbook example of madness.

As 1999 drew to a close, I was far from the only observer who could not understand internet-related share prices. Another observer was Mark Slater (son of Jim). With his father in attendance he assembled a board of experts in technology companies and their management and offered to the market an AIM-listed vehicle, Internet Indirect. Its purpose was to allow large investors who had to have some of their funds invested in Internet stocks a readily comprehended exposure to this sector.

The original issued share capital when the company came to market was 60m shares at 5p. Put another way, just £3m was raised. As it happens, this was largely provided by Slater family interests. Mark also took options to subscribe at 5p over a further 40m shares.

On the first day of trading, the stock instantly opened up at around 50p. So, a few days later, Mark raised more capital at around 40p. It should be understood that Internet Indirect had not yet made any investment of any nature in Internet stocks. It had merely announced that that was its intention. A few days later the stock was at 75p.

However, institutions still craved for more and so were offered a further 200m shares at 35p. They took it. There was still no sign of an investment in an Internet stock by Internet Indirect.

By this time, tangible net asset value, all cash, was 20p per share. It meant that the company could be liquidated at this point and that the original investors, principally the Slaters, could make four times their money – although, of course, Mark's options would make infinitely more since he had no need to put down the cash required to subscribe for capital.

Eventually, Iinternt Indirect arranged a bid for itself. It only lived about four months. It never had an office. It just had a registered office. It had made just a handful of small investments funded from the interest received on its cash pile.

Some felt aggrieved that they had paid 50p and 75p per share. But Mark Slater was never under any obligation to make an Internet investment at any time during his stewardship of Internet Indirect if he was not convinced of the wisdom of such an investment. Indeed, arguably, he was under an obligation to wait for calmer times since no value whatsoever was available during Internet Indirect's short life.

This was not a cynical exercise to milk the market. It was merely a vehicle that was made available to the market in terms of its entirely lawful prospectus. It merely responded to the climate of the time. Markets are always about perception.

Back to Cash

You may wonder what has happened to my cash investments in my pension portfolio. Well, they are still sitting in cash – after all, I take my own forecasts very seriously indeed. But a curious thing has happened in that I suspect that they have nonetheless outperformed FTSE. As I now illustrate.

When I cashed up one of my policies in 1996 I advised the pension company to see that all subsequent contributions were also held in cash. They confirmed that that was exactly what they would do. I had been invested in something called GT Worldwide Units – or one of these funds that one has not got the slightest idea as to what it is – I was only in it because of the tax relief on entering. The following years brought the usual annual statements, which I never read since they are so fantastically boring. They merely provided evidence that the pension provider might still be solvent – after all, it had obviously paid the postage.

That said, I could not understand why the fund seemed to be doing so badly given that, being cash, it could not go down in value. Although it was described as GT Worldwide Units, I presumed that it was some sort of cash fund and I therefore understandably expected the valuation to

51

reflect interest credited plus the subsequent annual contributions less the fund managers' charges (these are extremely irritating – I wish HM Government could get on and stop the wholesale theft in which these pension providers indulge). But after five years there really seemed to me to be a gap between expectation and reality. So I got hold of the pension provider and asked what was going on. Sure enough, they had simply continued with GT Worldwide Units, an equity fund, and ignored my cash stipulation. Immediately they recognised and reversed their error and the value of my holding rose 25%. This rather persuades me that the true underlying performance of broadly based equities from 1996 has been lousy. Given the distortions that accompany the construction of indices, perhaps I should not be wholly surprised.

Pension Policies in General

For want of anywhere else to slot in this opinion, I now remark that it is one of the observations of early childhood that the elderly typically cannot earn sufficient money to support themselves. It is therefore obvious to all but the brain dead that it is wisest to put aside sufficient lolly for one's old age. But the government takes away the necessity of grasping this essential truth (it argues that the working class is simply too stupid to do anything about saving for old age) and gives tax relief to those who save in certain approved forms. Unfortunately, the benefits accrue largely to those who would have saved in any event. And, at the time of writing, the working class shows no sign of stirring itself to save for old age. It will therefore in all probability live on state handouts twenty and more years hence. I think this brings the entire pensions encouragement legislation into question.

All this makes me wonder whether it is wise to leave large sums in government controlled and identified accounts ready to be sequestered at the whim of a politician. On balance, I think one should buy pensions policies. But I have no great confidence in the wisdom of such a remark.

The guru of market madness

History always repeats itself. For dot.com madness in 1999 read radio madness in 1927 or railway madness in the 1840s. You can always learn from the masters and hence I now turn to ROASO, short for *Reminiscences Of A Stock Operator* by Edwin Lefevre, published in 1923 – now available from John Wiley and Sons. Lefevre was a journalist and picked up on the story of Jesse Livermore, the stock operator in question and referred to as Lawrence Livingston in ROASO. Livermore committed suicide in 1940 – his funds had run out. It is recorded that he suffered from depression - then not recognised a s an illness.

Livermore was born around 1880 and by 1895 found himself in bucket shops in North East America and eventually unable to trade since he judged the next movement in stock prices simply on the basis of frequency and direction of previous "prints" on the "tape": For younger readers some sort of explanation of these two terms is demanded and here offered.

As it happens I also am too young to claim intimate knowledge of 1895 bucket shops. But my interpretation of the ROASO bucket shop is as follows: every time a stock traded on the NYSE the price at which trade occurred was noted and sent out by wire and printed on the "tape" issued from a "ticker tape" machine which presumably kept on ticking. Recipients of these price advices in (say) Poughkeepsie did not know whether the next "print" would be up or down and were therefore prepared to bet on it by buying (or selling in the case of the reverse approach) the last print plus one eighth of a dollar. A further dollar (or more, if wished) was put down as stop loss. So a purchaser of Union Pacific might pay $90.125 after a print of $90 by putting up cash of $1.125 per share. In this example, as soon as the tape printed 89 or a lower figure, the punter was wiped out but had no further liability. Correspondingly the punter could run the position as long as he wanted until he elected to accept the last print available as the closing bargain. I presume these contracts were daily bets. Lefevre does not say.

Livermore was clearly one of the first chartists. He judged volume from frequency of figures and charted price movements in his head. He was so successful that the bucket shops upped his premium from $0.125 to eventually $1. So he had to give up and try his hand in a broker's office in New York.

Livermore makes several broad judgements. One is that one cannot beat the market. But he does not explain it very well because he does not say what he means or why this is so. I think he means that the cost of staying long or short of the market for many years is quite high – at least 3% over base rate on the long tack and possibly 4% on the short tack. (It will be understood here that base rate is reckoned to be equal to the rate of return on the market expressed as capital appreciation plus dividends – for if it were otherwise there would be an imbalance as between the choice of cash or the market.)

I disagree with Livermore. I think one can occasionally take a strong view of the market and beat it. An example that springs to mind was the peak of the Internet boom, which occurred in March 2000. Another example was the grotesquely oversold condition of the market some days after the twin towers attack. But it is not easy to judge these moments in the middle of the battle. For instance I myself had a tremendous opportunity to trouser at least £1.5m net of tax on 21st September 2001 through closing my (far too) many shorts. Indeed, I told all who telephoned that it was time to buy to close. But I did not do so myself since I was aiming for a FTSE level of 2500 and not the 4300 at which it stood. I failed.

The general conclusion is that one should confine oneself to individual stocks – indeed, that seems to have been how Livermore made his most successful moves. ROASO is obligatory reading for any investor. It would be reproduced here if I were free so to do.

WHEN & WHAT TO SHORT

"I never loved a dear Gazelle –
Nor anything that cost me much:
High prices profit those who sell
But why should I be fond of such?"
Lewis Caroll, Phantasmagoria, 1911

Stock selection and timing of sales

I am not sure why a short-seller is referred to as an investor. After all, he does not own the stock. He is really a disinvestor. But, and by extension, to refer to short-sale stock selection as stock deselection suggests a process whereby one ceases to be interested in a stock - when quite the reverse is required. Arguably, a stock disinvestor should really also be a very small (one share, actually) investor in the same stock - this is the only means of ensuring that one receives copies of annual reports and notices of meetings. Thus, and strictly speaking, one should be simultaneously a stock selector and deselector. Strange but true.

Enough of semantics. The problem is to find the stock to short-sell. And the only way of which I am aware is to be an avid follower of fashion. This does not mean adopting flared trousers either pre- or post-1970. It means watching the market go barmy with excess on the up tack. This can go on for very long periods. Quite obviously Asil Nadir and his Polly Peck International were riding for a fall if the conduct of his close associates ten years prior to PPI's eventual collapse in 1990 was any guide. But ten years is a very long period in which to stay short. It would be far too costly in dealing and handling expenses even to contemplate. So all that one can do is to note a stock as eligible for a short-sale. One should keep a list and maintain files on all such stocks.

I wish I could pass on the sure means of identifying the moment (in advance of its occurrence) when the fashion fades, but published or prospective press comment is invaluable. If you reckon that a story is seriously damaging to the profit/cash flow prospects of a company, you must also make the judgement as to whether others will share your view, either immediately as you place your order or in due course. If immediately, will they sell at the same time as you (in which case, you may yet have to "pull" or cancel the order on the grounds that their short-term selling will have occurred by the time your order is completed) or will they sell after you in due course so ensuring a superfluity of stock in market-makers' hands to enable you to buy back your position? And will they sell so long after you that superfluity of stock is achieved only after you are compelled by logic or market practice to close your position? You must decide very quickly and on the balance of the probabilities. This is not for those who hesitate or have poor judgement.

Technically, selling a week or two before the publication of results is a sound approach - provided one is reasonably confident that the results and accompanying statement will serve one's purpose. This is not as easy as it sounds. Long before the insider trading legislation ever came on to the statute book, I assisted in the establishment and recruitment of staff for a new company. An obvious opportunity was for me to sell shares in the quoted company from which the staff were largely derived. In fact, the interim results, which came shortly after my sale, made no allusion to the departures, which were nonetheless common knowledge in the trade. It took a further nine months before the full year results formally declared the commercial disaster. It was then that the shares halved. However, some eight months previously, I had to close my short position at a loss of the order of 10% - stamp duty was then 2% which made a loss rather more likely.

As I recall matters, the only consolation was that the broking firm (now, and not surprisingly, defunct) through whom I sold, took my failure to deliver stock as proof that they had lost the certificate and, anxious to maintain their reputation, sent me a cheque for sale proceeds as if I had so delivered. Not even a telephone call from myself to advise their error had any effect. Again, selling in advance of press comment is very attractive provided one reckons that one knows what the journalist in question thinks. This is also not as easy as it sounds. Contrary to the opinion held by some, journalists do not give away the content of forthcoming articles. For theirs is a tough life and indiscretion loses a scoop or, at any rate, a claim to originality. Further, as Hilaire Belloc so sensibly remarked, you cannot bribe or twist the British journalist. You can certainly give him a free lunch. But, as anyone who has tried it will confirm, to demand of a journalist that a free lunch compels a puff in favour of the luncheon host invites a swift riposte.

So, and on balance, there is only one way to win the confidence of a journalist and that is to do his work for him. You must find the facts that are new and not understood by the market and, in my opinion, it helps enormously to draft the essential sentences of the article. This skill comes about with time, experience and hard work. I offer no short cut to success here. You must be quite certain that bad advice or, worse, untrue advice to a journalist will cause one to be struck from his presence and that of his colleagues.

Although there are clauses in the Financial Services Act 1986 that strike me as bordering upon the insane (and we should be clear that the Blue Arrow fraud trial, based on the FSA 1986, convicted subsequently-acquitted people and deeply damaged their careers without a brass farthing being paid by HM Government in compensation) there are curious side advantages undreamt of by those who drafted the legislation. I am thinking here of those sections which seek to inhibit market manipulation. They are draconian and, in practice, only capable of quixotic application. The result is that capable research analysts at stockbroking firms are increasingly reluctant to be quoted in the press or even to run the risk of being thought to have briefed the press for fear of encountering a regulator on the rampage. As a result, it is the case that, from time to time, their only channel of communication is through a person whose career and livelihood cannot be ruined by a regulator. This can be you. However, I cannot offer any advice as to a gracious process whereby one can ingratiate oneself with such informants. Further, there is the serious risk that the source may misadvise you. After all, he may not owe you a duty of care. You will just have to take matters step by step. Persistence will pay off. Good manners and humour eventually open all the world's doors.

Avoid Trains!

The choice of what to short-sell is always difficult. It is even harder when the chosen target is loved by the market. Oh, to be sure, after all the buying has been done (or shall we say when the loving has been done?) the only direction for the share price is down since sellers are bound to dominate. The trouble is that it is very hard to know when all the buying has been done. So the first rule is that a short-seller, who aims to stay alive, DOES NOT STAND IN FRONT OF TRAINS. Because, if he does, he will very probably get hurt. If you doubt that proposition, think about it this way: say The Lord of Misrule were standing with you beside a railway track and five miles away you could see a train chuffing towards you. And let us just say that at that point TLOM said "I'll give you £100,000 provided you chain yourself across the track. This is not really a test of your nerve since I happen to know that, with only a hundred yards to go, the train will stutter to a halt. I know this since I know the stoker forgot to put in enough coal for his journey. Indeed, I even paid him £10 to forget." Well, I think you get my drift – unless you are a very trusting fellow, I think you would decline TLOM's kind offer.

IT IS EXACTLY THE SAME WITH STOCKS AND SHARES.

I illustrate this by remarking that those who shorted Internet stocks in 1999 were typically burnt to a cinder. Curiously, in the long term, their decision to sell has proved right. It's just a small matter of timing that train. Per contra, I think the best stock to sell is one that has been kicked over the edge of the cliff. Because, when that occurs, there are lots of kind-hearted people who, trying to extend their love affair, catch (for which, read buy) it. It is then that you sell the stock. Perhaps one might put it another way: at that point you are pushing the train back down knowing that its momentum is on your side. And, incidentally, it is best practice to sell when the others are bouncing it up by buying for recovery. This takes self-control and patience.

I used to reckon as a rule of thumb that it was worth selling over-geared stocks such as (for instance) property companies with far too much debt as the property market boiled over. But old age has made me more selective and less energetic. It seems to me to be much wiser to keep a file of a company's accounts and statements (Company REFS is invaluable) knowing that the stock is fundamentally overvalued and then to wait for an announcement of interim or final results, having sold short a few days before. It is always possible that the directors and the company's public relations advisers do not present an entirely accurate picture at the point of the announcement. But usually they do (after all, it is a criminal offence deliberately to mislead the market) and the truth will out. Provided the financial journalists are doing their job, the share price should sink.

On stock selection, I make one other very important point: why compete against people who are very well informed and where they can earn vast sums of brokerage pursuing their point of view? I refer, of course, to institutional stockbrokers covering FTSE 100 constituents. Very occasionally, one can see an opportunity to short FTSE 100 stocks but, generally, it cannot be worth the effort to look for opportunity here.

Profit Warnings
I am not sure why a company's first profit warning is nearly invariably not the last. But, like London buses, profit warnings rarely arrive in anything less than threes. If I had to explain, I would remark that it takes years to build up the momentum of a really good company but, once a setback occurs, the management are, so to speak, put on the back foot. It just is not easy to regain momentum.

In some cases, it is not a question of regaining anything since there was never much to start with. A tremendous example of that is BTR (now part of Invensys), which by 1991 had just acquired Hawker Siddeley and had achieved a remarkable run of results for many years. But BTR's approach was to acquire companies and, on accounting for the acquisition, raise credit balances to meet reorganisation expenses – the resultant goodwill debit was simply written off to shareholders funds – and nobody seemed to mind. Eventually, of course, there were no credit balances left and the true performance of BTR had to be seen for what it was – rather pedestrian. The result has been a share price, which is a twentieth of its peak in 1991 – I guess that the FTSE 100 index had risen 200% over the same period. So, on a relative strength basis, BTR stood at one sixtieth of its high. That is quite a fall. Please note that the clever fellow, Sir Owen Green, who built up BTR, had had the foresight to retire in 1991.

Since I have elsewhere advised that shorting FTSE 100 companies is a poor use of one's time (I merely referred to BTR because it is a high-profile illustration), one should really confine one's cynicism to stocks that are practically handled. A good example of these would be high technology stocks. For, when these disappoint, they really disappoint. Marconi, Energis, need I say more? Typically, these creatures have no asset base to support the share price in times of trouble. Indeed, they are entirely based on exciting prospects. So it follows that, if the excitement is announced as deferred or, worst of all, cancelled, there is virtually no chance of the share price recovering its verve. It often pays to wait for such an announcement and then short-sell. This is because most investors cannot bring themselves instantly to recognise on the announcement that they have been had. These investors have to buy again "to average down" or whatever. You should sell them some stock.

Companies that Whinge

From time to time company managements have whinged at adverse comments about their companies' prospects. Without exception their shares have subsequently declined – particular when legal action is threatened. This is because no undervalued company ever remains unappreciated indefinitely and it is therefore wholly unnecessary to threaten the use of lawyers. Where a whinge is complimented by defamation proceedings it is an absolute certainty that the management has something to hide and aggressive short-selling is therefore in order.

During my brief stint at UK-iNvest I managed to generate quite a bit of whingeing. This was largely because UK-iNvest.com was run by cowards and so it was soon widely known that they would cave in to any threat. One company that whinged very loudly was the gold explorer

Minmet which threatened both myself and Tom Winnifrith with legal action because of an article I had written. I cannot think why Tom was mentioned in the legal letter from Minmet other than that he had written elsewhere how overvalued this stock was. Anyhow Minmet was then 22p. It is now 12p. The moral of the story: if a company starts bleating – sell.

Fiddling figures to suit a bull market

During bull markets, investors suspend disbelief since they wish to get in on the action. The result is that managements are frequently tempted to fiddle their accounts so to massage the results to show a better face. Of course, it all comes out in the end and, when it does, the denouement is much more marked. But, as a rule of thumb, one should never hold shares in a company which is fiddling its figures and one should prepare to short-sell stock when bad news starts to emerge.

General Market Conditions

As it happens, I started my accountancy practice in 1975, sorting out the management accounting side of a firm of estate agents in Hampstead. As a result, I came to meet many of the lessees of the properties managed. One of them was Alfred Marks, chairman of the employment bureau of that name. He was a very agreeable fellow – or, at least, he was to me. In early 1976 I ventured to remark to him that his company must have been having an unhappy time what with the general unemployment and so forth. He knew that my drift was stock market related but warned me that I should be careful about shorting his stock. It stood at 10p. The following day Adecco, a Swiss company, bid 40p cash. Had I been short, I would have been well and truly roasted.

And this illustrates an important general point. Shorting is a piece of cake when the market has topped out and is getting on with its decline – the famous "slope of hope" (preceded, of course, by the "wall of fear" to describe the climb to the top). But there comes a point when stocks cannot be shorted with impunity since there is nobody else left to sell stock after one has sold. In such circumstances, stocks can be massively undervalued – as, I think, my experience of Alfred Marks shows.

Further, it is not possible to arrange for some sensible fellow to mark one's card as to the turning point. One is obliged to note the turn of sentiment oneself. And when it comes one must deal fearlessly. Virtually everybody cannot.

Fraud and fraudsters

Fraud is more widespread than one might at first suppose. It is practised by many allegedly respectable people - perhaps clearing bankers, for instance. For, as is well known, depositors at UK clearing banks could never withdraw all their savings if they were all to choose to withdraw them at the same time. Of course, this is a most unlikely embarrassment for the Government of the day because depositors with UK clearing banks are most unlikely so to behave. But it can be reasonably argued that the majority of depositors are the victims of a confidence trick. They have been "conned" into depositing their cash in the belief that they can have it back at any time they choose. Society tolerates this state of affairs because it reckons that it can live with it.

Well! Are clearing bankers alone in this behaviour? Most certainly not! For instance, I might be invited to lunch and telephone my host with the advice "I'll see you at Wiltons at one o'clock sharp". What I really mean is "I'll see you at Wiltons at one o'clock provided I do not have a heart attack on the way there". But, if one were to qualify all such acceptances in this manner, one would expend a disproportionate amount of time to no effect. Time does not permit the expression of truth. Society accepts this. Confidence is vital in any commercial operation. He who cannot muster it need not bother to commence trading. It is really an expression of "I'm me. Trust me". All reasonable people recognise the wisdom of that presentation by a trader. After all, even if one has never traded oneself, one has many times attended the theatre and been transported by acting. One has seen something achieved.

Criminal law penalises deception ("obtaining a pecuniary advantage through deception") where on balance another could be or has been hurt. And there is the problem: how does one determine the balance? After all, as we have seen, nearly all takers of credit in commerce deceive. The real question is the degree to which they have so behaved: has their behaviour been reasonable in relation to those who have extended credit? And, actually (as you may be relieved to learn) most do not find this a difficult problem in practice. However, there are some who do. Leaving aside those who are tempted to desperate actions in the terminal period of a business, there are people who are born or moulded in childhood to deceive or consumed with the need to take revenge upon their fellow citizens through deceit. It is partly that it saves quite a lot of hard work. After all, what could be simpler than advising the customer that the work has been done (when it has not and where the customer may take some years to find out the truth) and then rendering an invoice for settlement?

And then there is the derivation of pleasure: there is no doubt to my mind that a principal motivation to deceive is the pleasure derived for the deceiver. I have known an entrepreneur and his accountant operate for five years some twenty bank accounts (all at different branches of some five or so banks and in respect of twenty companies) cross-firing cheques simply to borrow about £100,000 in total against uncleared effects. As those of you who have not previously contemplated such conduct can appreciate, it entails an hour or so a day to work out and check each balance and frequent use of couriers to meet deadlines. The process has to continue every single business day of the year. It means that there is no such thing as a holiday. It entails massive bank charges. It entails drawing sudden short-term loans from (say) pawnbrokers to satisfy any bank employee who has come to wonder about the account. It is truly an engagement with hell. The only possible result is ultimate impoverishment. And the only possible motivation to persist with it (I am convinced that the fraudster had several opportunities to wind up the scheme) was a pleasure derived from it.

Is there any sure way of detecting a fraudster if one is merely an observer of an entrepreneur and his company? I doubt it. There are merely pointers. But a way to initiate the process of review is to consider whether you can ever get a straight answer to a straight question. In my experience, fraudsters have a unique ability to change the subject. They may bully the questioner or they may charm him. It does not matter how the questioner is deflected. The fact that deflection is practised is the important point. A really competent fraudster devises a grand lie to support his act. This lie is so monstrous that it is accepted. Maxwell devised his "charitable" foundation, hidden in Liechtenstein, to control his commercial interests. Had he merely had a family investment holding company, resident and operated in the UK, many of his transactions would have been seen for what they were. But, by putting them offshore and giving them the cloak of some higher purpose beyond mere commerce, they came to be accepted. After all, not merely could he claim to be working for charity, he could show modesty by deferring to trustees. Of course, the audience was never in a position to check the claims. They went unchecked.

Another fraud is to devise a special fervour, which is peculiar to the fraudster's company. For instance, about twenty-five years ago, an office equipment company (whose name I forget) established quite a stockmarket reputation because its staff never used Christian names but addressed one another as Mr. Brown or Miss Smith or whatever. This manner of conduct was put about as evidence of high formality and moral rectitude. Actually, it was a cover for massive deception - the casual enquirer would typically learn nothing. Put another way, it meant that any outsider dealing with the staff found some special performance laid on which precluded the reasonable person's understanding of the staff and the company. The general conclusion on the long tack is that one should beware of investing in any company that one does not understand. An extremely successful dealer whom I have known for many years always declines to invest in electronic companies because he does not understand electronics. Not even IBM is sufficiently large and seemingly endowed with momentum to tempt him to reconsider his stance. In short, he consciously declines to run the risk of being conned. For the short-seller, the message is clear: as soon as a company is inexplicable, doubt it and put it on the short list. In the majority of cases, you will get a trading opportunity. Of course, you may have to wait some years because top class fraudsters have an astonishing tenacity to maintain the deception.

Essentially, the British are a forgiving lot. For instance, I and two colleagues lately tried to propose to some 1,100 shareholders of an Internet company, whose accounts and conduct offered extensive circumstantial evidence of fraud, that management changes were immediately required. Perhaps I do not sufficiently look like an earnest tecchie to appeal to such investors. But the fact is that I failed to deter these shareholders. Insolvency has now occurred.

Fraudsters are, of course, well aware of the public's forgiving nature. And they take advantage of it for all it is worth. One of their best opportunities arises on the separation of the general location of the shareholders from the point whereat the company's operations may be minutely viewed and understood. Distant mines in far off lands are therefore the best scam vehicles. Here the promoters achieve a double whammy. The first is that (I do not apologise for repeating this long-standing saw) a mine is a hole in the ground with a liar standing next to it. That is the investors' first hurdle. The second is that if the mine itself is hundreds of miles into the middle of inhospitable territory such as, to take a current example, war-torn Angola, there is zero chance that any shareholder will choose to turn up to check the operations. This is a perfect setting for fraudsters and those generally inclined to over-promote. All that is required is a willingness on the part of investors to suspend disbelief. This suspension often occurs closer home with high technology companies, which the investor does not understand and merely accepts as sound on the word of another. The fallout from the current crop of Internet flotations promises to be pretty bloody. Although not for those who are short at the appropriate moment.

One problem about over-promotion, from the point of view of the promoter at least, is that cash never lies. If a promoter causes his promotion vehicle to sell to a seemingly flush customer, who does not pay on time, it may well be the case that a profit is booked. The problem is that the cash does not turn up. Balance sheets always reveal this. Forgiving investors overlook this problem. But you do not have to. Remember: the cash is or is not there in black and white. (One can never rule out a forged bank statement or the bizarre claim by the promoter that £5m is actually in the bank when it most certainly is not – this occurred four years ago with Display.IT which I have covered later as a fraud.

The booking of profit can be most mysteriously handled. Take for example the December 1997 accounts of Pickquick PLC, a golf-training equipment promotion. These were signed off in mid February 1998. Yet Pickquick's only sale (circa £500,000) of any consequence in 1997 was quite properly disclosed in the 1997 accounts as being to a related party, which was a company in Hong Kong, controlled by one of Pickquick's directors. Pickquick's supplier to enable the sale was a factory just over the border in Mainland China – I never checked whether any goods had been made and delivered - was cancelled a few days after the accounts were signed. This did not stop investors from subscribing a few weeks later for further new capital at a cost of twenty times the original subscription price. As I say, British investors are a forgiving lot.

Incidentally, Pickquick was one of the first times that Tom Winnifrith and I collaborated. Ranged against us were some of Fleet Street's finest who, suitably wined and dined, swore that the equipment was a real winner. I am sure their lucky readers are truly grateful.

It's Promotion Time

I have frequently heard managements who are really just stock promoters refer to the "management of expectations". This is a really cynical process. Essentially, it entails releasing information to the market by one avenue and then releasing more by a different avenue at a later date. You may ask: why the change of avenue? Quite simply, those who are party to the original avenue and considering the second are bound to ask why the further information was not released at the original release session. After all, it had been available for release. Meanwhile those attending the second avenue, usually selected because they are not intimately acquainted with the conduct of the information-release through the first avenue, fondly imagine that they have has got a new and better handle on the story and prompt a further wave of investors to try their luck. And so on. This cynicism on the part of the promoters can lead to changes in brokers. It follows that a change of broker is a point to query.

Development of trading strategy

I have no strong views on strategy. It is not possible to confine oneself to short-selling when a bear market is certainly to hand. One must merely await the moment and never overplay one's hand. This is much harder than it seems.

Timing of opening short positions in general

While it is important only to short-sell a stock that is clearly materially overvalued and which will be seen as such by the market after you, yet within the time required, there is no alternative to weak market conditions for optimum success. I have heard it said that one makes more money in a bear market than in a bull market. One reason I suppose is that exposure to the market can be roughly three times one's long position - depending upon one's collateral requirements. It therefore follows that a 20% decline in share prices in general will yield rather more to you as an investor than a 20% rise. But the reason is more complicated than that. For, although a continuing and well-entrenched bear market will take leaders down by *25%* or more, it usually occurs at a time of contracting credit and economic confidence. In such circumstances, the number of companies that can move on to the short list to be sold increases rapidly. The chances of an insolvency rise rapidly. Bankers lose their nerve. Investors readily despair and decline rights issues that would be quite feasible in normal market conditions. Finally, most investors will not short-sell and, like mesmerised rabbits in front of headlights, will not even sell positions that are glaringly overvalued until the brutal truth emerges. The scenario is a killing field for the bold, decisive and level-headed. The trouble is that it is such fun that one tends to forget that a settled time (the usual condition) can return unseen and be costly to cover. The conclusion is simple: if the market really breaks down, instantly accelerate your sales. And, the moment it stabilises, cut your short losses in general and be extremely selective about running any short position. Arguably, you should not have more than three serious short positions open at any time because you otherwise run the risk of your concentration and sense of relationship to the positions wandering.

As I write I have 45 short positions open. As a rule, do as I say not as I do.

Investment models

This is not a book about investment analysis. But I think that it is important that one should hold accounts of targets. I start with REFS and then refer to the published accounts. One should have a good idea of factors such as Price Earnings Ratios for the target's sector and gearing that may prove acceptable (or not) to the market. Further, there are clear instances in the recent past when accounting practices offered the opportunity for a company to delude investors over many years. Certainly, "acquisition accounting" produced overstatement of profits for many companies until very recently (when a fresh, if different, set of absurdities has started to emerge).

The chapter that covers Maxwell Communication Corporation includes the note prepared in my office in respect of MCC. It shows that acquisition accounting obscured some important truths about MCC - although, and in fairness, the adjustments that could and should have been made by investors stared out of MCC's own accounts. For myself, I am not dogmatic about accounting standards. Even if they were to cost nothing to implement and audit, they are merely part of the language of business. And, since I would always argue that the purpose of language is to serve the user - even to the point where truth is purely a subsidiary or incidental objective, it follows (for me) that most time spent seeking perfection of accounting standards is time that is wasted. I would be impressed if the search for such perfection could be shown to reduce the incidence of fraud or encourage capital markets to operate more efficiently or cause business managers to apply funds to new projects on a more informed basis. But, since I see very little evidence (if any) of that, I would advocate saving the money spent on the search and subsequent changes, particularly as this money is currently levied in effect by a monopoly (because the companies that are audited cannot avoid audit and accounting standards).

You can skip this paragraph if you wish but, as a small digression, it seems to me that conflict is liberty. What this means is that by seeking to win an argument one prepares one's ground and thus reviews all one's strengths, weaknesses and opportunities. This process engenders liberty. Arguably, applying finer and finer standards in accounting constitutes the same beneficial process of achieving liberty. And politicians are duty bound to arrange such a process for their people. It is just that the selection of the field of conflict can be to economic advantage. Accountancy products cannot be eaten and do not fall within this category.

The influence of the press and other commentators
Whether one is considering buying, buying to close, selling or short-selling, one has to be conscious of what the market is thinking (and then try to do the opposite or avoid following the crowd). As it happens I take all the UK quality press with the exception of the *Guardian*. I was about to add that, whatever the numerous shortcomings that may be identified in the *Guardian*, for a short-seller, it is, of course, extraordinarily well written. But that would be to miss the point: which is that ever since the widely-reviled Rupert Murdoch decamped to Wapping, the quality UK press has improved beyond recognition with the possible exception of *The Times*. This improvement is also found in the financial pages. Inevitably, opinions there recorded affect share prices - particularly in active markets when punters are ready to follow the recommendations of newspapers.

I do not care to be dogmatic about the effect of other sources. For instance, when Cazenove decide on a view, they move the market through their trading. But they are not indiscreet. So they are not a source. Others are indiscreet when they should not be and so it has to be decided whether they are in breach of their obligations to their clients. If they are, one is legally as well as honour bound not to take advantage of their indiscretion. If they persist in being indiscreet, it makes you wonder whether they intend ultimately to deceive - a different proposition altogether!

I have taken tipsheets in my time. But the real advantage of a tipsheet is to draw one's attention to an idea for further investigation or to enable one to go against the trend of the tipsheet so to close one's position. He who follows tipsheets to the letter will simply go bust or steadily waste his capital. However, whether the information comes in written or oral form, it needs to be studied and weighed for quality and influence. For instance, take a market report column in spring 1995 which contained the advice that a certain firm of brokers considered that Tadpole Technology should be sold at 120p (the price was then 98p). The casual investor might remark that he should buy the stock on the grounds that it should not be sold until it is 120p. Of course, he might decide a moment later that his dealing expenses would be disproportionate to the limited upside he would here be considering. However, a reflective investor would surely decide that it is a rather odd firm of brokers that has clients holding the stock and yet which publicly limits their profits or recoveries. Accordingly, he will surely conclude that the brokers are probably really declaring that there is little upside and that the stock is quite possibly to be sold - particularly to those who are sufficiently ill-advised to buy (for whatever reason - one of which may be the suggestion that 120p is the selling point). I appreciate that all this may seem rather devious. But short-sellers who fail to engage in textual analysis will lose money.

Newspaper articles can be written in a perfectly responsible way. An example is Michael Walters' article recommending Queen's Moat Houses (QMH) dated Monday, 22 May 1995. It was a perfectly fair and enthusiastic recommendation for what was in reality a very long-dated warrant at a seemingly low price. The article itself was part of a series that Michael has been writing for publication each Monday morning in the *Daily Mail*. Unsurprisingly, this series built up a considerable following over the years although it now no longer appears. Equally unsurprisingly, private clients stormed in to buy Queens Moat shares. By the end of that Monday they had more than doubled to 18.5p on volume of 37m - and it must be understood that they had been relisted the preceding Thursday at an opening price of 3p (to close at 6p) and had continued up another 3p on the Friday - volume was tens of millions on both days.

I reflected upon the facts and read Tuesday's press which even suggested that some of the buying the previous day had been prompted by "corporate activity" (for which read takeover or long-term stakebuilding purposes). All this seemed rather silly to me because, in all probability, any "corporate activity" deal could have taken place during the preceding three months - after all, Queens Moat had been reconstructed over the preceding three years. It would be rather odd for the bidder to show his hand as soon as relisting had occurred. So that reason seemed to me to have caused misinformed buying on the Tuesday morning. But I also judged that the public occasionally loves an investment name that has made it money in the past and/or where losses are to be recovered. Queens Moat clearly fell within that category. So buyers were misjudging on that account.

Finally, Michael's article said BUY at 9p. It did not say BUY at 20p. And I am quite certain that Michael would never recommend buying a stock which had doubled on a Thursday, gone up by a further 50% on the Friday, and doubled yet again on the following Monday, if he were writing a column for publication on the following Tuesday. It was as clear an example of the crowd having gone mad as one could hope to identify in a typical year's trading. Further, there was a real bid by the market for stock. So, on behalf of myself and others, I short sold over one million Queens Moat at 19.5p and 20p. Within another fortnight, I had trousered over £50,000 profit. I swear to you that this was not difficult save in so far that there was an irritating delay through checking the conversion terms of part of the debt where, as it happens, I did not have a copy of the relisting documentation to hand.

EVIL'S BOASTS

"When a man says that his word is his bond...take his bond."
- Evil Knievil, 2001.

It is always hard to find a fraud and to remember that one might have made a mistake as one plunges to gather the harvest of one's forecasting ability. But it is thrilling to realise that the market has been had and that death awaits the stock. The best that I can recall since 1995 are Display.IT, Lanica Trust (Lanica did not die – it just shrunk – and how) and Equisure. Pan Andean was not a fraud but it was a tremendous opportunity. I have revisited Access Satellite, Maxwell, Polly Peck and Spring Ram largely for old times' sake and have also boasted about my triumphs in shorting the (non frauds) at Ashtead and Baltimore.

In the past, I have exposed frauds via a column in Sunday Business and thereafter on the website UK-iNvest but I fear that most editors are too timorous to hire bears these days. Companies – and their lawyers – are far less likely to kick up a stink when faced with a soggy buy puff than when faced with a stinging sell note. These days my only outlet is via a fortnightly webcast on the Internet site www.t1ps.com.

DISPLAY.IT - the textbook fraud

In mid to late 1996, a friend mentioned that he had bought a few shares in Display.IT at the equivalent of 20p (in due course, there was a five for one split – but I here ignore that and confine myself to one set of values to avoid confusion). Display.IT purported to be a financial information services provider with a difference in that it circumvented the need to use Reuters or Bloomberg (services which cost then and still cost something of the order of $25,000 p.a.). The Display.IT customer had merely to pay USD100 or so and slot in the Display.IT disk and, hey presto, the user's PC was ready to take financial prices off the net in real time.

It was not emphasised that there were in practice substantial further costs to the user by way of stock exchange fees. Nor was it stressed that the disc did not work properly since, as will become clear, these were rather subsidiary considerations. Certainly, when I was told of this service I thought that some miraculous and patented opportunity for the consumer had arisen and it was on that basis that I visited Display.IT's offices in Cannon Street to listen to Peter Levin, the boss, spell it out. I was completely fooled.

So it was that a few weeks later I wrote an extremely bullish article for my column on the original Sunday Business (then controlled by Luke Johnson). For Levin had explained that although sales were relatively slight in this country they were charging ahead in Germany and the US. This was of course another variation of a fraudulently promoted company's operations being elsewhere than where the investor can check claims.

By then, Display.IT was capitalised at around £100m and looked capable of making £20m p.a. a year out and a further £40m another year later. £100m looked a steal and the shares accordingly sat at 630p – having visited 800p.

It was a day or two later that I was lunching with Jim Slater who heard all this and then suggested that I ask myself the same questions again that I had asked Levin and see if I came up with the same answers. Needless to add, I had a Pauline conversion. It was obvious that I could not see anybody at the Cannon Street offices since there was nobody there. It was obvious why the sales to Warburgs had not materialised since the IT manager thought the discs were no good. It was obvious that a friend who had tried the disc thought it was no good – despite buying the equipment specified as ideal by DIT – since the disc was indeed no good. It was obvious that the equipment servicing department/customer query service had no address and only occasionally answered the telephone since, in fact, there was no such department – merely a fellow paid to act as if there was one.

So I sold tens of thousands of shares on behalf of myself and others. It was a no brainer. DIT was quoted on Ofex which is often thought of as a market but which is in fact a dealing facility operated by J P Jenkins. At the time there was quite a trade in DIT and it was relatively easy to sell stock since JPJ had buyers on the other side – in practice these buyers were chums of Levin acting to keep their fantasy going and spurred on by Levin's assurance that Cawkwell was a complete fool and that he was going to get terribly burnt.

Things might have remained there for an irritating period during which I might have been compelled to buy back to close had it not been for a remarkable breakthrough. Levin claimed that DIT had sold a block of disk licences for USD11.5m to Alsina, a company in Luxembourg, which would take over the European distribution of the licences and, most importantly, pay DIT this very sum forthwith. Needless to add the shares recovered their poise after that and it was beginning to look a little squeezy for me and mine.

However, a journalist pal interviewed Levin in front of a reliable witness and where Levin confirmed the figures for the Luxembourg deal and advised that the investors behind Alsina remained confidential but that one of them was Ross Perot, the Texan founder of EDS and presidential hopeful. This was the lead that I required. A solicitor known to me drafted a suitable letter to Perot and I got the reply I really needed when Perot's office stated that Perot was frequently claimed to be associated with fraudulent promotions but that this was the largest yet.

Not that I particularly care about those defrauded by Levin, I nonetheless took it upon myself to report his conduct to the DTI eighteen months after DIT had gone bust – just to see if they would do anything. It transpired that by then Levin had departed for the US. A fellow from the Serious Fraud Squad visited me (Why on earth take such trouble? What's wrong with a telephone call?) and advised that government's chief concern was the money laundering behind the financing of DIT. Why they could not be bothered to deal in good time with the most blatant and persistent breaches of S47 of the Financial Services Act 1986 that I have ever encountered is utterly beyond me.

Lanica Trust
Lanica started life as The New Guernsey Investment Trust and by the

time it came to my notice had approximately £3m in cash in its balance sheet and nothing else. However, the interesting feature was that it was capitalised at around £100m. A dealer, one Andrew Regan, had persuaded various institutions to take stakes in Lanica as a condition of their providing mezzanine finance for Lanica to take over substantial operating assets of the Co-op. Quite how a £100m capitalisation is achieved in these circumstances is and was beyond me. So, naturally, I sold it short. I took the trouble to write a piece in my Sunday Business column and, I believe as a result of this and various other expressions of astonishment, the LSE suspended the quotation. The effect of that was to remove a public valuation of the very currency which Regan was trying to offer for his schemes.

Thereafter, matters developed into pure farce with directors of the Co-op meeting Regan's men in motorway cafes to hand over confidential documents which Regan knew or ought to have known were not theirs to release. Two directors subsequently got the sack. Their defence would be that the Co-op was only heading downhill and that it would be best to get on with breaking up the organisation while there was something to break up. Although I sympathise with their stance, they had nonetheless contracted with the Co-op's members to put such a point of view to them rather than to anybody else in the first instance.

Equisure
The American Stock Exchange is respectable but, somehow, some guy decided to use that exchange when repeating a fraud in 1997 he had successfully pulled off (he was successful in not going to prison – others, however, did) about five years before. He formed a reinsurance company, Equisure, and floated it on Amex. The director's forecast was for steadily rising earnings. This was not difficult since Equisure's only customer was an insurer, which in turn had only one customer, a metals trading group shipping between South Africa and Europe. The unusual feature here was that all three companies were controlled by the same directors. Thus the directors had only to type out the results and release them to Amex once a quarter. Successful trading was wholly irrelevant.

Audit was superfluous since there was so little to audit. And the directors took the precaution of appointing an auditor based in Milwaukee – or somewhere equally absurd – for a company that operated in Belgium. When I telephoned the auditor and asked him whether he had ever visited his client's premises he advised that he had not. I told him that he ought to get along as soon as possible. Not that there would have been much point since the Belgian police raided the joint a couple of days later.

There is always doubt attaching to a decision to short since only a bighead can claim to know exactly who is buying on the other side. But I rather felt that since Equisure's finance director had been in a French gaol at all material times that was a risk I would just have to take. It happens.

Equisure is yet another example of the fraudulent use of a venture far away from the shareholder base – so to avoid common sense scrutiny. It works best with resource stocks but here worked a treat with an exclusively American stock distribution programme declining to check a rather humdrum office building in Brussels.

Striking Lucky – Pan Andean Resources
Pan Andean was a huge hoot – although the conduct of the authorities was wholly contemptible and irrelevant. Pan was capitalised at around 40m shares at 5p and was a vehicle for some sweet-talking Irishmen to drill for oil in Bolivia. They contracted BHP as their drilling partner.
As the summer of 1996 wore on the stock spiralled up to over 100p. I mentioned to the *Daily Mail* that all this seemed inherently improbable but was advised that (i) although the drilling was down to a level of 15,000 feet, insect life at the surface was consistent with the proposition that oil (formed some 50 million years ago) was to be found and (ii) the reason no oil was to be found during the drilling was that the drill itself was so modern and close fitting to the rock that traces of oil could not get on to the drill piece itself – the fact that there was no oil was just too obvious an explanation.

And so it came that after a long and most agreeable Friday lunch a broker and I resolved to short-sell Pan to the Irish market. At the time the Irish liked to buy Pan Andean for the weekend so that they could read about it in their Sunday papers and take a profit on Monday – there is a risk to this policy in that, not merely might no story appear, there might be no oil. Verb sap. But the broker is a professional fellow and decided that it would be much wiser to telephone a BHP high up on the lowdown. He failed until Monday evening when he got through to some office or other in Bolivia and was advised that the drilling team "had left town already, Senor". This rather suggested that the well was dry.

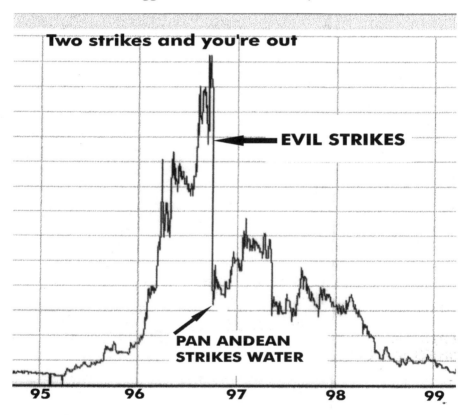

So he sold for me and others at about 100p in a manner verging on the demented – after all it is rare indeed to be able to short-sell virtually free of risk. The snag was that a fellow in my broker's Manchester office took it upon himself to buy a lot of this stock since he reckoned that he knew PA inside out. It does look odd when a firm is simultaneously selling and buying the same stock for different clients, particularly when the buyers in

this instance looked in their *Daily Mail* for the following day and read that
I and my broker were celebrating Pan Andean's collapse which of course
occurred as soon as a Pan director stepped off the plane from Bolivia at
Heathrow, found himself asked to explain Pan's share price weakness and
was so obliged to disclose that the well was indeed dry.

Sensible ordinary folk would normally applaud my broker's diligent
enquiries (as my friend, Roland Shaw, who founded and chaired Premier
Oil for thirty years, said *"He just rang the goddam guy up and asked him whether
it was a dry well"* – the implication being that it was open to anybody
so to telephone – which it was). But – you guessed it – the authorities,
hypocritical and Clouseau-like to the last, blundered into the act by
initiating all sorts of enquiries which started with my broker being sacked
from his firm when, of course, it was the conceit of the Manchester man
that should have been punished.

Access Satellite
Access Satellite was the first bear-raid that I ever developed in any
organised sense. It arose because, in early 1986, I was asked by a client
of my office as to the feasibility of buying operating assets of Access
Satellite. This company was developed from a shell company, Morland
Securities, which had itself originally been known as Malaysian Tin Mining
Company. It specialised in a mobile "work platform" which enabled its
users to reduce or eliminate the use of scaffolding. Seemingly, the cost of
the platform could be rapidly recovered through saving the capital tied up
in conventional scaffolding and, of course, the heavy labour costs incurred
through putting such scaffolding up and taking it down. Although
I understand that this platform has now achieved some acceptance,
particularly in North America, by 1986 it was only marginally appealing.
In fact I understand that SGB, the well-known scaffolding company, had
turned it down before its design was ever taken up by Access Satellite. I
do not know why. But, at the time, it seemed strange to me that a potential
major beneficiary from this product which also had the expertise to
evaluate it should not have adopted it.

However, I had noted the flotation of Access Satellite a few years previously and the adverse press criticism which accompanied it and which had advised that the trading record was altogether too short to allow a proper judgement. But I had then decided that it was far too premature to take any steps on the short tack. Besides, at that stage of its life, the promoter had yet to sell his shares and it seemed very likely to me that Montagu Loebl Stanley, the company's brokers, would take a positive stance towards the company.

It was sheer coincidence that my client approached me about Access Satellite. And, as it happens, it was clear to me that there was no business to be done by me with Access Satellite on behalf of my client. So I asked him whether I was free to short-sell the stock (arguing that I would not have thought of doing so without his having raised the possibility). In fact, I offered him the first sale and thus the first bite of the cherry - he declined, preferring some other fruit, no doubt. There were about 15 million shares in issue and the stock had declined from its high of £3+ to, then, about £1.20.

The market size was in about 15,000 shares on a 2p spread, which was acceptable in terms of dealing cost limits. I sold 15,000 shares. It was then that I had an attack of doubt and stayed my hand. This was foolish because the best time to sell is at the outset of a move -not when the stock has moved to confirm one's judgement. Anyway, the price slipped about 5p and by then I had had an opportunity to study the accounts. Although the company, audited by KPMG Peat Marwick (no less), was making money, it was consuming cash since the profits were tied up in debtors. It occurred to me that the debtors were not settling their accounts because they might have had some difficulty in satisfying themselves that the goods were of merchantable quality.

Further, it had been pointed out to me that there were one or two very large debtors whose failure to settle at all could prove seriously embarrassing. Not merely would the profit record disappear but an insolvent position would probably emerge. I also bore in mind that this company might have a degree of "pig and pork" in attendance to explain the high level of debtors. "Pig and pork", incidentally, is the process whereby Pig Limited buys from Pork Limited apparently at arm's length when in fact there is undisclosed common ownership of both companies. The result is that profits emerge in Pork Limited so that Pork Limited's bankers are conned into financing, in effect, both companies. The auditors cannot systematically pick it up. And the only financial cure for both companies is that Pig Limited ultimately disposes of that which it has purchased at a profit after covering the warehousing costs incurred. Needless to add, this cure is not usually to hand in time. The practice is fraudulent.

I was then advised that my client, quite separately from his original deal, would sue Access Satellite. This was really all I needed to talk quite confidently to those who would listen. As a result, the shares started to ease down a little faster. I contacted Barbara Conway, who had a column in the *Daily Telegraph,* called "Scrutineer". Sadly, she died prematurely of cancer a few years ago. She was gutsy and had a clear head. I drew her attention to features of the company and she published. This made the shares even soggier. I even offered her a ticket to Boston, Massachusetts to attend the submission of evidence in open court: she declined - she already had enough to publish.

By now I had attracted the attention of Access Satellite's management who had understandably identified me as a nuisance. They and their brokers issued a reassuring statement and, for a day or two, my position became rather squeezy. You may well imagine that if one has sold 100,000 shares in lots of 5,000 or so at a time because the bid has been so weak, the process of reacquiring these shares can be just as protracted and very expensive as the price climbs away from one.

In fact, I later learnt that the directors had purchased 500,000 shares (about 3% of the issued equity) simply to keep the price up in the face of stale bulls departing the scene and, also, the short-sellers who had got stuck in. It made no difference, the share price just would not recover its verve. I then hit on the brainwave of approaching one of the partners of the Access Satellite managing director's brokers. I asked him to ask his client whether he would grant me a traditional put option at a cost of

25p to sell 200,000 Access Satellite shares at 90p within the normal three months.

In effect, the managing director would have an opportunity to buy 200,000 Access Satellite shares at 65p. His broker asked me for forty-eight hours to think about it. You may therefore imagine my surprise when a few hours later and long before the forty-eight hours' time limit had expired a chap who I guessed was the director in question and a colleague (whom I took to be a potential witness in any defamation action that might be conceived) breezed unannounced into my office in Jermyn Street, London with a request to see me alone. I consented. They demanded to know for whom I was acting. I declined to tell them. I then asked them who they were. They declined to tell me. I asked whether I could take a photograph of them with my Polaroid (I said this was kept in my secretary's drawer - I did not say that the drawer in question was at her home - for the best effect would thus have been lost.) They declined. We then agreed that there was no more to say. Of course, they had said everything. One telephone call confirmed that I had been talking to the managing director. No managing director who is entirely sane would have dreamt of behaving that way and then failing to disclose his identity. An hour or two later, his broker telephoned to advise that his client was not interested in granting the put option. From there on, it was open season and suspension followed a few days later.

There is a postscript. It covers a technicality. A friend had sold, at my urging, 2,000 Access Satellite shares through his broker at around £1. Since the shares were suspended, he had asked me to ask around for stock. I found exactly 2,000 shares with Smith Brothers (now Merrill Lynch) at 12p apiece. I bought them through my (a different) broker. But, after two months, Smith had not delivered stock. It only then transpired that the 2,000 that Smith were due to deliver were the very same that my friend had sold them. No wonder they could not deliver. In effect, the matter was sorted out by Smith sending my friend a cheque for 2,000 times 88p. But it is a good illustration of the general point that in the stockmarket you need to keep an open and alert mind.

Polly Peck International

As it happens I had a rather torrid financial time from October 1987 to mid-1990. My firm's overheads were radically increased through a rent review occurring at the peak of the property boom. Further, billings by my firm were deferred or cancelled through the sharp decline of business confidence. To make matters even worse, one or two of the small limited companies that were the bread and butter of my firm's business went bust as the credit squeeze bit. That meant bad debts for me and permanently lost sales. Although the Government was to continue being dramatically foolish through keeping the UK within the ERM until September 1992, my escape from this folly came about by chance.

In mid-1990, Asil Nadir, Polly Peck's charismatic boss, realised that the game could be up and approached a major US bank for finance (of the order of £1.5 billion) to engineer a "management buy-out". This was still quite fashionable then because the banks still hankered after the vast profits derived through the fees charged for such arrangements even though the credit climate had obviously changed to an altogether quieter affair. In the event, Nadir's proposed lending bank appointed private detectives to check out Nadir. A friend of mine came to hear of points that this enquiry revealed. And if it had not been so serious it would have been laughable. The further rumour arose that Nadir was "cashing and newing" his Polly Peck stock at the end of each account. Such conduct constitutes borrowing at a staggering rate of interest. And it means that either the borrower is mad (and should be avoided) or that he has run out of money (which raises the question as to why) and may well be engaged in a share support operation both to improve collateral values and/or enhance share marketing possibilities.

I concluded that Nadir was not mad and was therefore behaving in this manner through desperation. As it happened he did announce a management buy-out, which temporarily caught the market on the hop. However, the evidence that the funds were in place to support the announcement simply was not there. From then on it was plain sailing. Besides, a friend with good eyesight saw police cars prominently proceeding to Berkeley Square and Polly Peck's HQ. My financial affairs were righted. With the benefit of hindsight I can only stress that Nadir had a hypnotic effect upon many.

Maxwell Communication Corporation

As some readers will know, the collapse of Maxwell made me both financially and personally. So I remain extremely grateful to Robert Maxwell. (Others are entitled to remain less charitably disposed.)

The Polly Peck profit was in the bag by late September 1990. And, although the credit climate was still puncturing reputation after reputation, it never occurred to me that there could be something bigger and better than Polly Peck. How wrong I was. For most readers, the Maxwell life story has been recited too often to justify its inclusion here on anything other than on an outline basis. He was born in Czechoslovakia and first entered British consciousness with his rank of captain right at the end of the Second World War. He would then have been about 22 years old. He picked up a Military Cross. This established him as brave. But his business career was one confidence trick after another. By 1980, he had ceased to be a Labour MP and was widely mistrusted and disliked. For instance, Sir Sigmund Warburg opined that Maxwell had betrayed his fellow Jews through his misconduct. But Maxwell frequently deployed lawyers to issue gagging writs and, as a result, the truth as to his nature was not generally known.

So, in the early 1980s, he managed to save British Printing Corporation (itself created in the late 1960s by a strikingly ambitious fraudster). Maxwell just bullied the print unions into submission. This outcome was long overdue. No one had hitherto had the guts to do it. It is sobering to reflect that had the unions not been so obstructive they would probably have ended up with a management that would not have stolen their members' pension fund. As a result of this coup, the banks warmed to Maxwell. And BPC (or Maxwell Communication Corporation as it subsequently became) blathered on through the 1980s.

By 1990, the balance sheet was crammed with intangibles - two major purchases in the US had produced that result. Further, Maxwell owed substantial debts secured on his shareholding in MCC, then valued at about £1 billion. But the shares were descending and thus the expected yield based on historic declarations was rising as investors scented a cut in the dividend. By October 1990, the indicated yield was of the order of 15% - or at least twice the general yield on FT-SE 100 stocks. That said, the announcement of the 31 March 1990 results confirmed the dividend and Maxwell himself announced that he would take shares in lieu of cash as his dividend because he believed so much in the company. He neglected to mention that there was no cash available with which to pay him a dividend and that he had persuaded the bankers to lend against the shares issued to him by way of dividend.

The birth of Evil Knievil
However, the cash actually being generated within MCC was a great deal less than extrapolations of the accounts indicated might be the case and informed investors had started to wonder just how representative of MCC the accounts could be taken to be.

My first sale was at £1.45. It was on 3 October 1990. The shares eased a little. It was then that a friend called at my office. In a brilliant brainstorming session he and I wrote a note about the accounts of Maxwell - it always helps to prepare a note to clarify one's mind. This note (which is reproduced in its entirety below) was simply a sober reflection upon truths. I wanted to fax it to all the market-makers in London to make quite certain that they would mark their offers down before I was obliged to close. My friend was not so sure - he was then better acquainted than I was with the provisions of the FSA 1986 and, in particular, S47 (which, incidentally, tends to stop truth emerging).

But I was not deterred and even though he would not sign the note I had to give it an authorship. Judging that it would be a little conceited to suggest that I alone was the author, rather than type my own name, I chose **Evil Knievil**.

Review of accounts of Maxwell Communication Corporation PLC
("MWC") for the year ended 31st March 1990, prepared by
Evil Knievil

SUMMARY

The reported profit for the year ended 31st March 1990 of
£101.1 million is   entirely attributable to the accounting
treatment of the company's acquisitions and disposals together with
non-recurring items.

The maintainable profits, and thus their expectation in future
years, are negligible. In effect, therefore, MWC has been paying
dividends out of capital. Accordingly, unsecured lenders should be
concerned at the level of cash dividend payments.

The disposals of shareholdings in Donohue   , Quebecor,
De La Rue and the Italian interests will be completed subsequent to
the half-year ended 30th September 1990*when US 410 million dollars
of debt repayment becomes due. Thus, MWC is likely to maintain the
interim dividend and the financial impact of the disposals will not
be fully known until the release of the figures for the year ending
31st March 1991 in mid 1991.   *and before 23rd October 1990

The market values of the underlying assets (which are mostly
intangible) are probably significantly below book value. Given the
very high level of debt,MWC shares offer little, if any, underlying
value. If the company were to default on interest or debt repayments
and were placed in administration, there would be little prospect of
any pay-out for shareholders.

NOTES

1. On consolidation of the acquisitions of Macmillan, OAG
and Merrill Publishing during the year ended 31st March 1990, MWC
revalued the fixed assets* to 'fair value' to the extent of £163.1
million above the cost of the acquisitions but also made provisions
for integration and reorganisation totalling £76.7 million which
were taken direct to reserves, i.e. not through the profit and loss
account. However, in the same year, MWC utilised provisions of £84.3
million which appear to have been credited through the profit and
loss account. On this basis, the reported profit before tax of
£172.3 million should be adjusted downwards by as much as £84.3
million. Attention is drawn to the Source and Application of Funds
Statement and to Note 29(b) to the Accounts.   *and investments

2. Other operating income of £47.9 million, sales of
publishing titles of £18.9 million and non-compete agreements of
£6.2 million have been deducted from operating costs. Particularly
interesting is 'other operating income' which is up by £40.2 million
over the previous year and includes £41.0 million profit on property
development and sale of property development companies; these are
clearly non-recurring items. In any event, the accounting treatment
of deducting these profits from operating costs distorts the analysis
of gross margins which the chairman claims have improved as a result
of the switch from low margin printing to higher margin publishing.

........2

85

3. Non-recurring net gains on sales of investments less
provisions of £18.3 million have been deducted from net interest
and investment income. See Note 7 to the Accounts.

4. The accounting treatment of the acquisition and subsequent
disposal of Maxwell Graphics illustrates that the financial statements
do not, in _ my opinion, give a true and fair view of the financial
position of the group. On acquisition of Maxwell Graphics, MWC wrote
off £199.3 million of goodwill direct to reserves, thereby reducing
the book value in the consolidated accounts. Subsequently, Maxwell
Graphics was sold at a profit of £24.6 million by relation to written
down book value and this amount was credited to profit and loss
account as an extraordinary item. This item, considered in the Report
of the Directors on page 29, is further detailed in Notes 4 and 9
to the Accounts. Note 4 advises that this treatment was in accordance
with the Group's accounting policy. The important issues raised by
this transaction are (a) the accounting treatment of writing off
goodwill in the case of Maxwell Graphics is surely inconsistent with
the accounting treatment adopted for the acquisitions of Macmillan,
OAG and Merrill Publishing - described in 1. above. (b) the extraordinary profit is a major component of the reported profit attributable to shareholders.

5. Since the acquisition of Macmillan, MWC has made several
disposals. However, in a number of instances,. the businesses have
been transferred to partnerships and associates at high book values
or MWC has received securities rather than cash. Thus, it is critical
to assess the value of the partnerships as well as these securities
held by MWC. For example, the sales of investments in the Michie
Company, Intertec and Webb Publishing in December 1988 yielded an
aggregate consideration of US 305 million dollars in respect of
which MWC received deferred loan notes with terms of 10 years and
coupons of 8 - 10 % p.a. * Were these loan notes disposed today, MWC
might receive US 200 million dollars or less and thus incur a loss
of the order of US 100 million dollars. *See Note 19 to the Accounts.

6. Another issue is the underlying value of the recently
formed Macmillan/McGraw-Hill partnership which is in the books at
£405.7 million - see Note 15 to the Accounts. The partnership
comprises businesses which were transferred at a very high book
value based on the following analysis: The partnership contributed
sales of £96.4 million and an operating profit of £5.6 million for
the period 21st July 1989 to 31st March 1990. Applying an earnings
multiple of, say, 13 times post tax annualised earnings, MWC's
interest in the partnership would command a market value of perhaps
£65 million, i.e. less than one sixth the value at which it appears
in these Accounts.

7. As a consequence of the accounting treatment for
acquisitions and disposals, the book value of the intangible assets
as a percentage of total assets is remarkably high and increasing
as a result of the announced disposal programme. As at 31st March
1990, intangible assets (excluding those in the Macmillan/McGraw-
Hill partnership) stood at £2.16 billion, representing more than
50% of gross assets and 215% of shareholders' equity at book value.
If the intangible assets attributable to Macmillan/McGraw-Hill
partnership are accounted for, intangible assets amount to £2.52
billion, representing 60% of gross assets and 250% of shareholders'

........3

equity.   In my opinion, it would be prudent
for MWC to write down the intangible assets by amortizing goodwill.
However, this would result in insufficent profit to pay a dividend -
and the dividend is, of course, supporting the share price at its
present level.

However, helpfully, the Annual Report and Accounts contains
Canadian Shareholder Information which reconciles the financial
statements to Canadian GAAP under which adjusted net earnings for
the year ended 31st March 1990 are shown to be a loss of £97.9
million compared to a reported profit before extraordinary items
of £126.8 million. Nearly all of the enormous difference may be
explained by the Canadian GAAP principle of amortization of goodwill,
resultant from acquisition,over ten years.

8. With adjustment of the non-recurring items and restating
the financial statements to reflect a conservative acquisition
accounting policy, MWC   made   a small loss compared with a
reported profit of £101.1 million - see schedule of Maintainable
Profits. If goodwill were amortized over ten years, the loss for the
year ended 31st March 1990 would have been £207 million or 33 pence
per share.

9. In its current financial situation, I consider MWC can
            no longer make large acquisitions and is now forced
to dispose assets to repay debt. As a result, MWC's reported profits
will fall dramatically and the company will not be able to maintain
its dividend.

MAINTAINABLE PROFITS

£'s million

	Reported profit: Year ended 31st March 1990	Adjustments	Maintainable Profits (predicated)
Sales	1,242.1	-	1,242.1
Operating costs	(1,006.1)	(156.4)[a]	(1,162.5)
Other income	-	32.0[b]	32.0
Share of partnership/associates	25.2	-	25.2
	261.2		136.8
Exceptional item	19.2	(19.2)	-
Total operating profit	280.4		136.8
Net interest and investment income	(108.1)	(18.3)[c]	126.4
Profit before tax	172.3		10.4
Tax	(34.5)		(3.6)[d]
Profit after tax	137.8		6.8
Minority interests	(11.0)		(11.0)
Extraordinary items	(25.7)		-
Profit attributable to ordinary shareholders	101.1		(4.2)

Notes: a. Operating costs adjusted for provisions utilised of £83.4 million, property dealing profits of £41.0 million and transfers to other income of £32.0 million.

b. Transfer ot other income of items deducted from cost of sales, being publishing titles (£18.9 million), non-compete agreements(£6.2 million) and other income excluding property dealing profits of £6.9 million.

c. Reversal of net gains on sales of investments less provisions.

d. Tax is assumed to be at 35%.

A few days later, a journalist on the *Sunday Times* enquired as to whether any one individual was responsible for the widespread nervousness in the MCC shares market. Of course, the simple answer is that nobody can be - nervousness is just a collective phenomenon. But, just for the hell of it, I remarked that the ringleader was called **Evil Knievil**. It made good copy. By then, Evil's note had been faxed round the City and Maxwell had got hold of a copy. It was immediately branded a dreadful slur - no doubt upon a "great and patriotic Englishman" or some comparable pomposity - why people were ever taken in by his style beats me.

If I had to guess, I would suggest that Maxwell always paid those who acted directly for him very well - after all, it was not his money. Quite a number of these people were respectable although, in effect, not extending credit to Maxwell. Further, they had no public duty to make known their personal feelings about their paymaster and, arguably, they had a professional duty not to make any comment at all. As a result, many others were fooled into thinking that Maxwell himself was respectable. It does not follow in logic. But that is how the human brain often behaves - it tends to judge a man by the company he keeps.

At the time, Maxwell had an undisclosed arrangement with Goldman Sachs such that that firm's market-making arm had every incentive to buy yet more shares - below you will find the print out which was obtained from MCC showing the positions of all the market-makers at around that time - you will note the staggering size of Goldman Sachs' long position. It was way beyond normal trading requirements. Further, as a market-maker one would have to be powerfully persuaded that the stock would rise to justify such a position. To this day, I do not know exactly what persuaded Goldman Sachs. I can, of course, guess.

On 12 October 1990, in London dealing hours, a broker, Peter Marks, of Branston and Gothard, (sometimes jocularly referred to as "Pickled and Ready", before its demise) sold stock to Goldman Sachs. He then asked the dealer to telephone him back. The record of that conversation is confused. But it was later alleged that Marks had informed the dealer that "Maxwell would file for bankruptcy in New York that night". Seemingly,

Goldman Sachs passed this on to Maxwell who then bullied the London Stock Exchange into making enquiries.

As a result, Marks was charged with a breach of S47 of the FSA 1986 on the grounds that he had spoken recklessly on a matter affecting the market. This was a serious charge because its prime effect could have been the destruction of Marks's career. I did not learn of this charge until January 1991 through a chance remark by a journalist whose principal purpose was to warn me that Maxwell had put two detectives on my trail and that, further, Maxwell had arranged for my telephone lines to be tapped. I do not know whether Maxwell ever took such a step - he was skilful at deviously disseminating through unwitting contacts the possibility that he might prove a threat - in this case, a colleague of the journalist who informed me may have been the means. I have always worked on the assumption that my telephones are tapped - any tappers hired by Maxwell must have had a thrilling time listening to my daughters booking tennis lessons and so on.

However, I was not to know what was actually happening in Maxwell's affairs. And, what with the Marks charge (which I knew to be defective because it could only be brought on the basis of evidence from Goldman Sachs - you will recall the secret agreement between that firm and Maxwell) and because I was repelled by the obsequious conduct of the LSE towards a proven bully and because of further points that were emerging, I redoubled my efforts to get to the bottom of the Maxwell matter. It was slightly a case of 'I'll get you before you get me'.

I should remark at this point that I had covered my short position in MCC at a small profit in late October 1990. This was because the price was not easing back. Instead it was showing remarkable resilience. Since I had only just escaped penury through the intervention of Polly Peck, I was in no mind to return to zero. I declined to run the risk. I also bore in mind the rule that, in a sense, the market is always eventually right. What this means in practice is that if the expected does not occur in the market, you must reflect on the possibility that you are wrong.

And, much to my surprise, the price of MCC forged up - eventually to £2.40. We know now that Maxwell, realising that his entire edifice depended on borrowings secured on his MCC stock, was stealing funds from MCC's employees' pension funds at an unprecedented rate so as to fund his purchases of MCC stock. At the time one could only guess the reason for the rise. It seemed wholly unjustified by the probable trading position.

Maxwell always confused his private with his publicly-quoted and shared interests. If you like, it was a clear case of "pig and pork" - see *Access Satellite*. However, one of his private interests was Mirror Group Newspapers (MGN). And, despite Maxwell's ridiculously erratic management of that business, it generated a lot of cash. Since his bankers had by January 1991 decided that they wanted their personal exposure to him repaid or reduced, he was compelled to float MGN. Needless to say, this was accompanied by the usual preposterous huffing and puffing. And he so forgot himself as to include in the press publicity process to promote the sale, the oral advice that the Mirror office buildings would also be sold. The drawbacks to this claim were that it was in public and, perhaps more importantly, the buildings could not possibly be thus sold - they belonged, in effect, to another. Of course, only a desperate businessman is so casual.

The Mirror flotation proceeded. The Americans particularly warmed to the idea - they rather like a chap with chutzpah - and, whatever one thought of Maxwell, he certainly had that. This was completed by May 1991 and the issue immediately went to a discount. The reason was obvious. The British market sensed that he would steal money from anywhere and that the Mirror Group and its pension funds would do just as nicely as MCC's notwithstanding the "ring-fencing" so carefully included in the prospectus. There had been a number of stories in the UK press concerning MCC's and other Maxwell interests' pensioners, both current and prospective, wondering how their future lives were to be financed.

Then there were whispers that Maxwell had stolen £60m through the acquisition of Tokyo Investment Trust. At the time, the acquisition was hard to explain - after all, what conceivable expertise could Maxwell bring to bear upon Far Eastern investment? But, a moment's reflection showed that the only purpose could be a desperate attempt at wrenching further cash from absolutely anywhere. It was time to reflect upon the fact that MCC's price was easing back from what was to prove its high for 1991 - £2.40.

Although the evidence of forthcoming insolvency was accumulating daily, I kept my mind ever open for more. This particularly arose through Maxwell's purchase in early 1991 of New York's *Daily News*. The owners were so disgruntled by the American print unions that they were prepared to pay Maxwell to take the company off their hands. Needless to add, this was manna from heaven as far as Maxwell was concerned and he motored his yacht *Lady Ghislaine* along the Hudson River. However, even though he may have been preposterous in his general behaviour, not even he could have justified his negotiating in New York while permanently and seriously drunk on brandy - and this was reported to me to be the case. The only conclusion was that Maxwell had finally gone mad. He was no longer remotely in charge of his destiny.

By mid-1991, some 25% of MCC stock was held by small investors for reasons of history. Either they had held BPC in the late 1960s or early 1970s or they had come aboard with Captain Maxwell. Such investors do not readily panic. Certainly, all UK institutional investors had left the party. As a result, it had taken relatively little buying by Maxwell's clandestine offshore fronts to hold the price up. But, of course, he was desperately short of cash notwithstanding the enhanced borrowings created by the rise in the collateral presented by MCC stock. So sellers outweighed buyers. And, as the price of MCC declined during the late summer and autumn of 1991, the banks which had lent on the security of collateral which was reducing in value could only be satisfied by sales of MCC stock. And the only effect of that had to be to compound the problem.

The last weeks of Maxwell's life have been well documented elsewhere. Roy Greenslade's excellent book *Maxwell's fall* published in 1992 by Simon and Schuster is especially good. So I shall desist from making further points.

However I will never forget the morning of 5 November 1991 and the breach of the chart point of £1.40 - where, it will be recalled, I had originally sold in October 1990. This was the point where the collateral decline became completely intolerable. As soon as stock was offered at £1.39 I knew that the game was all up and persuaded several friends to sell with aggression - something of the order of 1 million shares. The market took it in lots of 100,000 and the final sale at £1.25 was actually achieved in a lot of 10,000 only - the market was sated. That afternoon, Maxwell's death was announced.

The circumstances surrounding the flotation of MGN were the subject of a DTI enquiry published in 2001. I cannot begin to think why there was so great a delay between its being commissioned and being made available to the public. As I awaited publication I was minded to issue an all-embracing opinion by remarking that it was cowardice by hundreds of potential whistle-blowers that allowed Maxwell to ruin so many. No legislation will ever eliminate cowardice. That said, when the report eventually came out I judged that it was flawed by supposing that snitching on people is an every day act expected of all citizens in relation to all others. Peter Marks used my advice that there was no chance of the Crown's prosecution succeeding. He was, of course, acquitted. I still cannot fathom why the DTI ever brought the prosecution.

As far as I am aware, my review of the accounts of MCC (its trading screen abbreviation was MWG -to distinguish it from MCC, the cricket club just round the corner from my then home - whatever Maxwell was, he was not cricket in spirit) for the year ending 31 March 1990 was the first such review that was made publicly available. It was faxed and dispatched everywhere rather as the Samizdat press of the former communist countries. But many analysts deployed by the major brokers had come to the same conclusions. Their trouble was that they were inhibited by defamation law and commercial considerations from letting their views be known. Further, I know that one major clearing bank (defamation law precludes my naming the bank and thus identifying its cowardice and obsequiousness) sacked its broking subsidiary's media analyst for daring to speak his mind. Had I been one of its clients I would have slightly wondered what else this broking firm as agent, which owed me a duty of care, was suppressing.

I typed it out myself using, as you can see, a correcter ribbon. The ribbon was hard at work. But it was all worthwhile because Maxwell went incandescent when he read the review. It seemed then and it seems to me now to be pretty mild.

I do not know why *Evil Knievil,* the nom de guerre which was generally taken up by the press, first emerged from my typewriter as Evil Kinievil. I can only suppose that, in my mind, he was so evil, he had to be doubly evil. Then again, I do not know all the usages of "evil". For instance, my elder daughter currently advises that an invitation to tea can be "wicked". The printout of Sepon-registered holdings (page 95) in MCC shows the position that Goldman Sachs had built up as a consequence of the put option that
Maxwell had granted to them. I do not like Goldman Sachs since, in my opinion, they are not clubbable. It is true that not everybody would regard this as the acid test. But it will do for me and mine.

 I have resisted the temptation to reprint a copy of a newspaper annoucement of Maxwell's death. It is hardly ever wise to dance on someone's grave. Especially if his first burial was at sea.

```
MAX AA1548        Code MAX        MAXAA1548


SEPON LIMITED                              Shares      19,843,834

                                           212 Sent  / /
                                           Replied 21/11/90
THE STOCK EXCHANGE
LONDON                                     Reply Flag r
EC2N 1HP
                                           Update Flag

                                           Print Flag P



ÖáááááááááááááBeneficial NameááááááááááááááááááááááááááááááááááSharesááááááá
     GOLDMAN SACHS EQUITY SECURITIES (UK)              25,159,081
  °  MCLEAN (R A) & CO LTD                                  2,408
  °  AITKEN CAMPBELL & CO LTD                               1,374
F4CMDHELP ESCEXIT F2SAVE Sh-F1TABLE F3VIEW F7DEL F8MODIFY F9QBE F10MULTI




Nominee
Sub Record 653 on Line 8 of 16
  °  UBS PHILLIPS & DREW SECURITIES LTD                    40,768
  °  MORGAN STANLEY SECURITIES LTD                         35,286
  °  HOARE GOVETT SECURITIES LIMITED                       32,448
  °  NOMURA INTERNATIONAL LTD                              21,682
  °  SMITH NEW COURT SECURITIES PLC                       195,304
  °  S G WARBURG SECURITIES LTD                           126,692
  °  KLEINWORTH BENSON SECURITIES LTD                      58,493
  °  MAORGAN STANLEY SECURITIES LTD                         8,303
  °  DEWAAY SERVAIS & CIE S.C.S                             3,000
  °  LAWS & COMPANY LTD                                    12,500
  °  DISCOUNT BANK & TRUST COMPANY                         21,542
  °  S.G. WARBURG & CO LTD                                 30,000
  °  S.G. WARBURG SECURITIES (JAPAN) LTD                  100,000
âáááááááááááááááááááááááááááááááááááááááááááááááááááááááááááááááááááááááááááá




F4CMDHELP ESCEXIT F2SAVE Sh-F1TABLE F3VIEW F7DEL F8MODIFY F9QBE F10MULTI
```

This print-out of the Sepon-registered holdings in Maxwell Communication
Corporation shows the consequences of Goldman Sachs taking all stock
offered.

Spring Ram

The Ram of Spring Ram is derived from Mr. Rooney And Mr. Murray, the company's founders; and short-selling Spring Ram was colossal fun. One reason was that the maximum practical position to take was about 100,000 shares - the market would not happily deal at the touch in more and I was easily sufficiently solvent to cope with any vicissitudes that might arise on an exposure of the order of £125,000.

Unlike many other shorting operations, this started not so much from any particular words or use of words in the accounts although there were a number of most interesting points therein. It started with the sheer silliness of the December 1991 accounts, which was full of drawings of chaps sprinting off in running races. Well, I might have accepted this general sprinting off for excellence had the business been the manufacture or distribution of running shoes or of cream to prevent athlete's foot. But Spring Ram's business was builders' merchants' and DIY supplies. And, even though it is a sound policy for a company to use the glossiness of its accounts as an aid to sales- customers frequently warm to a supplier's claim to professionalism by reacting favourably to its accounts - there is a limit. Spring Ram's accounts were staggeringly and exaggeratedly glossy. To me, the presentation of the accounts looked to be trying to hide an altogether different state of affairs.

Further, a friend in the bathroom equipment business advised me that Spring Ram was slow to pay its bills. This should not happen in the case of a company that has tens of millions of pounds in cash in its balance sheet. Another friend, in the interior decoration business, advised me that he had always thought Spring Ram's margins wholly incredible since they were maintained and improved during the stiffest recession for some years. Accordingly, I reckoned that Spring Ram was a natural short-sell candidate.

I did not catch the top (it is always hard to catch either a top or a bottom), which was £1.81, achieved in May 1992. But my first sale was of *50,000* shares at £1.38 on 20 July 1992. Paul Murphy, who then wrote the market report for the *Daily Telegraph,* even reported that I, in concert with others, had picked my selling moment because Mr. Rooney had gone on holiday.

After all, given that Sir Winston Churchill opined that he could not think of a better time to kick a man than when he is down (this was in response to the plea that it would be the worst time) it follows that it is good practice to mount a bear-raid when there is no supremo around to give the best story in the company's support.

Actually, I did not get Rooney to take the mickey out of me (well, what else would you expect from a Rooney set upon restoring his name?). Instead, the *Daily Telegraph* market report was advised by the finance director, one Stuart Greenwood, that "the only thing to do with these so-called bear-raiders is to catch them and give them a quick kick in the knee". I put this down to a Yorkshireman's sense of repartee. So I sold another 75,000 shares - this time at £1.31. I put it about that I had purchased some knee-cap covers and a supply of Corton Charlemagne in case I were to find myself hospitalised.

Somehow, Paul got this story as well. I have elsewhere in this book considered how brokers support the share prices of their corporate clients. The economics justify their doing so. But this tendency causes even quite sensible stockbrokers to persist too long in support. And I must judge that this was the case over Spring Ram. A Mr. Pat O'Reilly of stockbrokers, Panmure Gordon, was then – he's dead now - a well-regarded judge of market affairs. But, for whatever reason, he declined publicly to admit the possibility that Spring Ram was doing less well than it was claiming. He said to the *Yorkshire Evening Post:*

"It's a seller's market at the moment. Spring Ram has been so successful in recent years that it has a number of rivals that would like to see it struggle. It's very easy for people to say that the company is struggling just because it isn't doing as well this year as in previous years. In fact, it is doing extremely well considering the economic climate."

The *Yorkshire Post* wrote: "One rogue dealer was reported to have wiped £30m off a Bradford firm's (i.e. Spring Ram's) value and made a packet". I take this reference to be to myself because of the newspaper's reference to "his having collected hundreds of thousands of pounds... Ratners and Brent Walker" - and that, however incorrect a description of what I had actually done, was derived from a *Sunday Times* article of eighteen months earlier - and that article was based on me. To me, it seems a lurid use of "rogue". Surely, the better word is "effective".

But the more interesting aspect of the article is the tenor of Mr. O'Reilly's remarks. One needs to be fairly careful before accepting points reported in this manner - although, in my experience, reporters are usually meticulous when reporting sources verbatim. First, although it was indeed a seller's market, it was not that much of a seller's market - sentiment was beginning to turn to the bull tack. And a broker of Mr. O'Reilly's experience knew or ought to have known that that was the case. So his opening remarks did not feel entirely right to me. There seemed to be a hidden agenda. Secondly, it is extraordinarily stupid to mislead the market on the bear tack because (i) it is a criminal act to do so - see the FSA 1986 S47 and (ii) there is little likelihood of profit - certainly by relation to that from perfectly readily identified over-promoted stocks elsewhere in the market. So, Mr. O'Reilly's remarks that the rumours surrounding Spring Ram could be attributed to jealous rivals did not seem sound. Jealous rivals might have spread them. But the rumours originated elsewhere. I discounted Mr. O'Reilly.

But I had bought to close at £1.24 on 23 July 1992 and, in a sense, was indifferent to the move back up as Panmure Gordon's clients purchased. So, on 27 July 1992, I sold 50,000 shares at £1.28. I do not want to bore readers with a blow by blow account. Suffice to say that although there was a useful profit the dealing expenses were phenomenal.

Although you might think that there was a steady decline in the share price of Spring Ram, the truth is that it oscillated quite considerably. After my purchase at £1.22 on 3 September, the price recovered to about £1.35 or more. However, in early November, Spring Ram finally announced the first of a series of warnings. This was referred to on 18 November by Paul Murphy in the *Daily Telegraph*:

"With an excruciating pun at the ready ('the silence of the Rams'), the bear-raiders are back stalking Spring Ram. They gave the stock a good spanking in late July, boldly

suggesting the home improvement firm had gone ex-growth and talking darkly of accounting irregularities. Sources at Spring Ram rubbished such talk at the time only to come clean earlier this month when the company launched a bid for Stag Furniture. Although the shares have lost more than 30% since the truth about problems at Spring's Balterley Bathrooms subsidiary emerged, the raiders reckon the management are getting off too lightly. Even loyal supporters of Spring Ram concede that some form of independent check on the accounts would help clear the air. The bears say that they are stunned at the board's indifference to the falling share price and are selling short in the belief that some parties in possession of accurate inside information are already off-loading stock."

Said it all, really. Spring Ram duly declined to the point of near extinction and has now departed the market. The fact is that, when a company is shown to be less than its claims, its share price performance is not merely as leaden as its contemporaries, it is usually much worse. Trouble is rarely cleaned up overnight.

Ashtead

Ashtead has been a remarkable short in that its decline has been long drawn out. I was introduced to the opportunity when contributing a weekly column in Sunday Business in 1997. My initial informant was a stockbroker who had been gagged by his employer - one of the major securities houses. Why do they do these things if they wish to develop and maintain a reputation for intellectual authority? He drew my attention to the lowish tax charge and the persistent year-by-year adverse cash flow.

There then followed two or three days telephoning plant industry sources and senior employees. With one exception, all were rather coy. I was therefore inhibited from publishing anything of note.

Ashtead's traditional response to at least one journalist who enquired about its accounts was (as Tom Winnifrith will testify) to threaten to involve lawyers. That was enough for me. I therefore shorted the stock from around 240p downwards. It has been a very long battle, fought over five years. Numerous profits warnings, later Ashtead stands at 30p and is still trading.

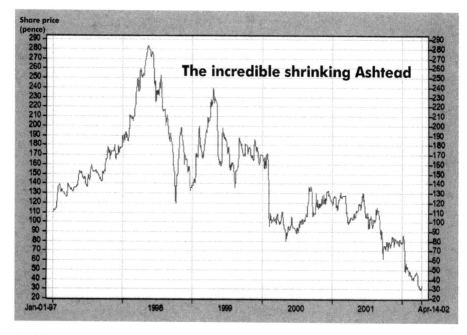

Share price (pence) — The incredible shrinking Ashtead

Incidentally the publication of "buy" notes from brokers who were also paid advisers to Ashtead suggesting that it would soon be undertaking a corporate review or getting involved in corporate action was another reason to go short. The brokers (Schroder Salomon Smith Barney in this case) would have been more persuasive had they discussed cash generation!

Baltimore

I suppose Baltimore was the greatest illusion of the tech bubble. Its shares were meandering around at £5 in its pre-bubble phase - although I for one could not understand what the business was or might be. It was then the punters took a shine to its Internet commerce solutions and ran it up to £150. This was the greatest momentum punt I have ever seen freely undertaken by sentient humans. It was quite normal to take on £500,000 worth of Baltimore to whip out £50,000 profit by lunchtime. And, for a while, that is exactly what happened.

It could not last and, in one final frenzied minute, it topped out at £150. At this level the company was capitalised at around £3bn. I still did not understand its business. But I could see that the bubble was punctured and, sure enough, it started to rattle back.

I mishandled the timing of my trades and, as a consequence, made a small fraction of the profit that I should have secured. However, the stock was split with ten new shares for each one held and, at 38p (or £3.80 in the old form), I was advised that it had no business and a cash burn rate that would surely extinguish its precious cash pile (there was no prospect of a rights issue). Today, Baltimore stands at 9p. It is taking time. But the dividend is at last coming regally to fruition.

As a general rule, if you do not understand an investment prepare to short it. There will always be a large number of gormless idiots who will have to sell after you so guaranteeing you a profit.

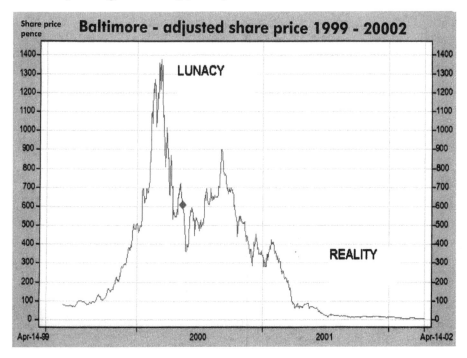

As a specific rule, if the maths does not stack up prepare to short it. At the height of Baltimore's market success, the market capitalisation given to the four biggest Internet security companies in the world was around

$21 billion. This is a highly fractured market with an endless number of small companies each attacking small niche sectors so to assume that the big four (of which Baltimore was one) would ever gain more than, say, a 50% market share would be generous. Yet – even when everyone assumed spectacular growth rates for sales of technology products (back in 1999), industry analysts argued that this entire market would be worth just $17 billion in sales by 2005. In other words the big four were trading on a multiple of just over two times the very best case sales forecasts for six years in the future!

Tom Winnifrith of t1ps.com used to trot out these numbers to audiences of investors around the country but for a while, at least, Baltimore et al defied all logic and gravity. These things cannot last.

THE TECHNICALITIES

"The world is made up for the most part of fools and knaves"
- George Villiers, Second Duke of Buckingham

In the US, short-selling is as common as supporting Manchester United is in the UK and, although many US short-sellers have the average brain power of the average supporter of that estimable football team, there are thousands who not merely take shorting very seriously, they are good at it. Put another way, there is competition.

Here in the UK, I doubt if there are more than a hundred punters who approach shorting in a methodical and substantial manner. It follows that should you decide to join this select band you are joining battle where there is little competition. I think it was Adam Smith who remarked two hundred years ago that should one gather some businessmen together it is only a matter of minutes before they try to construct a cartel. Well, I am not sure that Smith was right: if the total number of shorters by 2001 is one hundred and one, it slightly suggests that in some areas of commerce businessmen are slouches.

The New Regime and Opportunities

In 1997, GNI (part of Gerrard and National) started a service for serious private investors based on Contracts For Difference or CFD. Here, on the long tack, the investor purchases stock on the basis that he is merely marked to GNI's own position in relation to market-makers. There are two great virtues: the first is that no stamp duty is payable since the investor never takes delivery of the stock and the second is that, aside from the margin facilities offered, it is not necessary to have the broker, when seeking finance from the market, to pay the usually exorbitant price demanded by market-makers for implicit interest. Further, if the investor wishes to sell short, he is not confined to a mere 25 days. He can economically stay short for months without the huge expense of renewing the short position at the end of each week or two (and it should be borne in mind that the Stock Exchange will now only allow renewal of a short or long position on one occasion). On shorting, the stamp duty exemption also applies. The drawback is that this shorting facility is restricted to larger stocks since it is often hard or deemed poorly financially controlled from GNI's point of view to borrow stock in small companies. However, my reckoning is that all this is changing and that GNI itself will face competition in this field – thus offering short-sellers more choice.

Stock Borrowing

For some reason stock lenders reserve the right to ask for their stock back without notice and this can entail one having to buy one's position back at the wrong time. There is no way round this. Worse, when the attack on the World Trade Center occurred, stocks plunged such that a number of major stock lenders in the UK decided that they would cease lending stock lest they be accused of facilitating general stock market declines to the disadvantage of their policyholders and/or stockholders. This insane declaration that, in their not particularly humble opinion, the market was too low was accompanied by difficulties (greater expense and uncertainty) in borrowing stock all to the disadvantage of the stock lenders. It is what happens when childish and silly people are left in charge of the shop.

Size of Short Positions

You may find it very easy to sell some stock since, although the expected bargain size is much smaller than you actually encountered, the truth is that the buyer has a hearty appetite. Whereas you may count yourself fortunate in the short term, you may find that when you come to buy back, the buyer has not lost his appetite. As a result, you and he are competing for stock such that the price is squeezed up with disastrous results for you. There is only one means of avoiding this unhappy moment: you must not sell markedly more than the size – even if at the time of the sale you are convinced that the price is bound to slump.

SUSPENDED STOCKS
(WELL HIGH)

Suspended Stocks – The Mourning Story

Should you find yourself delightfully short of stock when a share price is suspended because of financial difficulties, you may well find that the suspension is permanent. As a result, you can seek to buy your position back from the market provided the bargain is solely from the market-maker to clear stock he may hold. But if the market has no stock you will have to buy it by private treaty from another holder. The best way to do this is acquire a copy of the register of shareholders from the registrar who is obliged to provide you with one within 10 business days of your request subject to your paying the necessary, which will vary according to the size of the register but typically be less than £100 for the average company.

You will then ring up directory enquiries and do your best to persuade the hapless holder to release stock. Here a certain diplomacy is required. Should one begin one's approach just a few days after the suspension with "I see that you are so stupid that you still hold Fraudulent Consolidated PLC. However, I am pleased to tell you that your agony is over, a tax loss established and the price of a lunch recovered if you'll just send your certificate and the duly signed transfer that I shall supply to P.O.Box Djibouti", one will tend to achieve relatively little. **There has to be a period of mourning by the aggrieved shareholder.**

So, on a suspension, although you may be extremely excited by all that lovely money being released to you, you should contain yourself and go off for at least a month's fishing (or whatever takes your fancy). When you get back, you should commence your programme of stock acquisition by gently sounding out some holding sizes that roughly fit and gently enquiring as to whether the holder would be interested in selling "having regard to tax losses". This mild approach is not overtly critical of the investor's bad judgement (or that of his stockbroker) and opens the way for sensible people to talk.

The liquidator of a company is obliged to keep the register open until his liquidation is completed. So, typically, you have at least a year and possibly some years to complete a purchase. But delay can lead to problems and I recommend two important pieces of advice (i) get your business done as soon as you reasonably can and (ii) get your broker to ensure that you can deliver stock sizes that are different from the stock sizes in which your sales actually occurred – for instance, if you have sold 10,000 shares and the only willing seller to you of suspended stock that you can find holds 12,500, make sure that the market will accept such delivery. The willing seller is asked to sign a transfer and send it and the stock to your broker who must pay the willing seller the agreed amount. In the alternative, you can trust the willing seller to bank your cheque and release the necessary documents. You then submit the transfer to the INLAND REVENUE STAMP DUTY OFFICE, WEST WING, BUSH HOUSE, STRAND, LONDON WC2 along with your cheque for the stamp duty due (0.5% of the agreed consideration). The transfer will then be returned to you. You then send it along with the willing seller's certificate to the registrar who will in turn reregister the stock in your name so allowing you to deliver stock to your broker and thus the market. I am afraid that this second approach is necessary where your broker declines to allow the willing seller to send stock direct to your broker for processing. This complexity arises through the Financial Services Act 1986 – after all, unravelling short positions should really go through market mechanisms. I really do not know why the law and its interpretation applies and I doubt if anybody else does.

Note that S127 of the Insolvency Act 1986 states that transfers of stock where a company is being compulsorily wound up must be approved by the Court. I think the idea is to protect a fraudulent company manager and owner of stock harvesting the remnants. But the effect of this law is costly delay and uncertainty and I very much doubt if it has any practical control of criminals. It is typical of incompetent meddling by the Conservatives.

Collateral

Since it is theoretically possible to lose an infinite sum of money when one has sold short (after all, one cannot know just what price holders will demand when it comes to buy back one's position), brokers are understandably conservative when opening short positions for investors, particularly private investors who may not always be available on the telephone when a really sharp movement occurs against them. Brokers therefore demand a deposit of cash and eligible stocks, preferably easily-marketed stocks such as FTSE 350 members, to support the short-seller's position. Typically, a collateral of 30% of a short position is required along with any unrealised losses. Brokers reserve the right to call for more collateral as soon as the first lot has been partially eaten into – even if only very slightly. It is very important to observe this rule. You will only otherwise find yourself being bought in.

Shorting Penny Stocks and Small Caps with a limited Free Float

Much below 10p it rapidly becomes much harder successfully to short a stock. This is because the spread is typically considerably greater in percentage terms than in higher-priced and more widely traded stocks. Further, there comes a point when the general supply of stock in a typically much reduced company is greatly constrained by the loss of interest in the share price on the part of potential sellers. So not merely must you pay significantly higher unit costs by way of expenses, you may simply be unable to buy at all at reasonable prices.

Finally, you may think a penny stock ludicrously overvalued. But it is possible for holders to hope far beyond reasonable expectation so that the decline in its share price that you anticipated before opening your short position cannot occur.

Shorting Nil Paid Rights and Warrants

You will note that compliance officers expect 30% collateral. However, since these fellows typically have virtually no experience of anything, let alone the stock market, it is possible to get "under the wire" by selling nil paid rights (which really have to be approached on a day trade basis) or warrants where one can get just as much exposure to risk for much less brokerage, stamp duty and, of course, collateral. You therefore need to keep a reference book of warrant conversion terms. One such, as a supplement to "Warrants Alert" published by the McHattie Group, has served me well. Where warrants can be converted at all times, it is quite often possible towards the very end of the life of the warrant to short-sell the ordinary and buy the warrant effecting conversion through the market or the registrar and so complete delivery on the short-sold position.

Shorting on Ofex

As it happens I greatly favour Ofex, the dealing facility run by J P Jenkins. It appeals to the libertarian in me. You will note that it is a dealing facility and most certainly not a market. Jenkins could improve this by ensuring competing market-makers in all stocks covered by Ofex. I do not expect they will – after all, a monopoly is good fun provided you are the beneficiary.

That said, there have been some stonking frauds promoted on Ofex and, were Jenkins minded to promote market-making competition on Ofex, I think these frauds could be much more readily seen for what they are: stonking frauds. Ofex has provided quotations for issuing houses, which are thus allowed to keep filtering dud stock into the unwitting hands of private investors. You might think that the DTI would object to this style of deception. Not a bit of it. The DTI to my certain personal knowledge is completely indifferent to anything important in this field of equity. I sometimes think that this is because they are idle. But, on reflection, the real reason is stupidity.

The opportunity arises for the short-seller in that he can sell on deferred (although not necessarily deferred) delivery dates and then fail to deliver since Ofex is not a stock market. Jenkins's solicitor will eventually write asking for stock if the stock price has gone up – and, in such circumstances, it is probably best to buy to close. But there is little incentive for the solicitor to write if the stock has gone down. So he does not. In fairness to your broker and Jenkins, all this can lead to strife. I really see it as a case of persuading Jenkins to show sufficient wisdom to clean up its act.

Opportunity Knocks – Rights Issues

Normally, there is no short-selling business arising during a rights issue period. However, every now and then, easy money is to be made. This is because the issuing house which has arranged underwriting is extremely concerned to see that stock does not get left with the underwriters and this is a real possibility should the cost of new stock be seen by the market as dearer than the old ex-rights-quoted stock. I illustrate: in late 1998, the sports goods retailer, JJB Sports, issued about £100m of new stock at 440p to fund an acquisition. Warburgs were in charge of getting the issue away. Unfortunately for them, if fortunately for me, the market lurched violently down so that an issue which was not all that attractive to start with was clearly priced above the market price that would apply after the issue closed.

But Warburgs, realising that, if they were not to support the issue price, the bulk of the issue would be left with the underwriters, held their market-maker's bid price at 440p with an offer price of 455p – all other market-makers kept their usual 15p spread but offered at 442p. The effect was to show the narrowest spread in JJB there had been for years. But, far better than that, the grotesque disparity in the bid persisted for hours and hours. It meant that a sale on T+15 terms – i.e. to a settlement date well after the issue closed – was virtually certain to be closed at a profit. Seemingly, Warburgs had a word with Merrill in the last hours before the issue closed because Merrill went on the bid with Warburgs a penny lower – the idea being to give the impression that there was a real bid independent of that offered by the issuing house behind the issue. This was not a particularly suave move since all other market-makers continued resolutely to offer stock at 442p. I'm sure Merrill and Warburgs are still good pals. A vast amount of stock was left with underwriters and it was simplicity to buy as much stock as one wanted at 350p or less a few days later. This was virtually a risk-free trade, which had the further distinction of being possible in size. Long live Warburgs.

Adjustment of requirements to close in the event of intervening scrip or rights issues

These adjustments are simply **a** matter of equitable sense. In the event of a scrip issue, when (say) a further share is issued for each one held, you simply need to deliver two shares for each one sold. Rights issues are a little more complicated. Here, you must buy nil paid rights to cover your sale contract. After all, the buyer of the cum rights stock that you sold has rights. And nobody bar you is going to ensure them. You buy them and deliver them to the market. But, if you do not, you will eventually be debited with the cost of fully paid new shares less the amount payable on subscription. Put another way, you will be "bought-in". Other things being equal, the ex-rights price will be at a discount roughly equal to the rights value.

And, while the cash profit available through buying to close the original sale is to hand on a T + 5 basis, the requirement for cash when buying nil paid rights is on a cash settlement basis. This means that you may be required to put up cash for which you had not otherwise budgeted. Further, it is generally best to leave the purchase of nil paid rights as late as possible. This is because there are always some investors who hold rights yet foolishly hope that some windfall will provide the cash to allow the new shares to be taken up. They tend to sell late. Another consideration is that the issuers of these new shares tend artificially to manipulate upwards the ex-rights price for as long as possible to encourage as many takers as possible and, no doubt, to reassure those who have underwritten the issue. However, this process comes to an end as the issue closes. It is at that moment that the most favourable buying opportunity may be expected to arise. I need hardly add that, sometimes, those who handle such an issue regard it as attractive and artificially manipulate the price down so that they can pick up shares cheaply at the end of the rights quotation period or through stock put on them as a result of the underwriting.

On balance, I favour buying nil paid rights in order to control the price paid. I dislike leaving a position open such that I am bought-in unless I am tolerably sure that there is a further fall to come - "renewing and cashing" would then apply. But you should not leave buying nil paid rights so late that the renounceable letter of allotment that you have bought cannot get through your broker's office to the market which originally bought your sale cum rights. You should discuss that with your broker.

There is a variation where new shares are issued in terms of an open offer and clawback. Here there is no trading of nil paid stock. The value of the right of a subscriber to the new stock is not transferable. However, if you have short-sold stock which is cum the right to participate in the open offer (the "ex-offer" quotation normally follows within twenty-four hours of the offer being announced), the buyer has a claim in the normal manner. Therefore he can insist that you deliver stock. He in turn must pay you what he would have paid by way of subscription. This is done through the market. There is a chance that he will not bother since the value achieved may be too small or potentially non-existent. It is entirely at his option.

Trading on Margin
Since the UK is a patronage bureaucrat socialist society it has an entirely inscrutable taxation system. One of the features of this inscrutability is that no deductibility is achieved in respect of interest paid on finance to buy stock – although the Revenue will happily tax gains on the stock thus financed. The only way round this is to classify oneself and behave as a trader in stock. Here one loses the annual CGT allowance but one achieves deduction for a range of costs which are incurred with a view to gain yet yield no deduction for capital gains tax.

There is another aspect of trading on margin in that there is nothing like investing your own money rather than the bank's or the broker's. This is because your cash compels clear thinking. As a result, many brokers will not let you trade on margin. In my own case, this strikes me as fatuous since I am quite happy to pay a reasonable rate of interest, observe margin rules and continue to syphon cash out of the market. And I do. But I think you ought to decide that this suits you before trying it yourself. It usually does not.

Spread Betting

As it happens, I lost £30,000 being short of Brian Lara runs in 1994. The effect was to put me off spread betting for a long time. Which I regret given that I now see it as the way forward for the sophisticated investor.

In a sense spread betting has been with us for centuries in that, on the old market floor, there were some rather sharp fellows, jobbers, now known as market-makers, who were approached by brokers seeking to deal in a particular stock. In theory each jobber was asked what price he was in the stock and what was his size. The price incorporated a spread. The spread was the jobber's turn and reflected the fact that the jobber did not know whether the broker was a buyer or a seller.

None of this is very important nowadays save that it is noted from fairly early on in life that there are always fatheads who know everything. And the fathead who says that he knows who will win whatever but who declines to contemplate failure on the part of his selection is just one of those things – a fool encountered in nature. So, in effect, spread prices allow for the reverse view. They give the response to the broker: you have my price – what do you want to do? The broker can reply that the spread is too wide and that he cannot be bothered to deal with that jobber. Or he can note the price but from his scouting round the market also note that the way he wishes to go is more cheaply available elsewhere. Or he can complete his business.

I am told that spread betting (on winning distances) started at the Prix de L'Arc de Triomphe in or around 1970. But I doubt that. For I am tolerably sure that two way prices on cricket runs were available in and around the LSE long before that.

IG Index was formed about 1975 and the IG stands for Investors' Gold. IG's founder, Stuart Wheeler, whose personal story I find quite remarkable if beyond the scope of this book, responded to the fact that UK residents could not buy gold without paying Vat thereon. The effect of this law was to make all trading in gold by UK residents quite impossible. IG just offered a two way price on gold, which was never delivered by either IG or the punter or investor.

In or around 1995 this approach was formally extended to cover not just financial futures in respect of currencies, commodities and indices (for so IG and others had developed and expanded) but also UK equities. Which is pretty well where we are today.

First, some general points:
Since a speculating investor expects to take more from the market out of his speculative positions than he gives to the market, he likes the fact that spread betting gains are free of tax. Since there is no tax relief for losses, such an investor may wish to confine his exposure to roughly half what he would risk in the market proper.

Spread betting firms typically only trade FTSE 350 shares. However, they will trade smaller shares if you ask politely and particularly if you leave large sums of cash by way of collateral with them. It is worth noting that there are now at least five spread betting firms engaged in financial betting and the number is rising as I write. So there is plenty of competition and I am sure that they will tend to expand the range of admissible stocks for trading purposes.

Now to the economics in the raw:
An investor telephones for a quote in a tech stock, here called (very originally) Techstock, yielding virtually no dividend (I have excluded the dividend for ease of illustration). The operative on the "shares" desk (why the term "equities" cannot be employed, I do not know) says the price of Techstock for settlement six months hence is based on the cash (i.e. current) price of 672p to 675p and assumes that the customer's enquiry is not in more than 5,000 shares (the maximum size at the "touch" price in the market) and is given 689p to 698p. The spread firm simply adds on 3p on either side of the touch price (there is a published scale – 6p in total applies to a stock whose mid price is from 500p to 699p) to give 669p

113

to 678p in the example and then jacks up each side of the quote by (say) 20p for interest at base rate plus 1% p.a. for five months. So the quote becomes 689p to 698p Please note that all stock market futures are priced to equal cash investments in that the future level of a stock market must equal current prices plus interest at base rate less dividends declared.

The reason that spread firms currently use 1% over base rate, rather than just base rate, for their internal purposes reflects their typical financing costs and the fact that investors generally tend to go long rather than short. But, of course it follows that those who are going short are getting an extra 1% p.a. over the six months or, in the case of Techstock in the above example, an extra 3p or so. If the shorter is able to persuade the spread firm to narrow its spread to 4p from 6p or 2p on the bid, he has in effect gone short at minus 1p brokerage. Yes, that is right: the spread firm has paid the investor to deal on his behalf.

Nor is it so bad on the buying tack. If an investor seeks to avoid stamp duty by going through CFD and to take advantage of leverage, he will receive perhaps 2% p.a. under LIBOR for his cash deposit and be charged 3% over LIBOR p.a. on the cost of his acquisition. At the end of five months the finance cost of perhaps 9% p.a. (or 2% p.a. greater than the spread firm) comes to around .6p more than that charged by a spread firm.

One final point of comparison: When the make up day arrives in December and the settlement figure is determined, the spread firm takes the middle price and deducts its spread, 3p in the case of our Techstock investor. However, should the CFD investor wish to close his position he must get the best bid in the market and then, typically, pay 0.2% brokerage. This entails a cost of market touch of 1.5p (it will be recalled that Techstock, priced at 672p to 675p, is on a 3p spread in the market) and brokerage of 1.5p or 3p all told. i.e. the cost to close is the same. But, given the financing cost advantage, the speculating investor whether going long or short, will find that spread firms offer better value.

It might therefore be wondered if spread firms do badly. And the answer to that is most definitely not. This is so since most investors open positions for settlement months forward (the maximum time possible and where the interest advantage on spread firms is maximised) but frequently close after a few days and, equally, most investors decline to deal in sums sufficiently large to enable the spread firm to reduce its spreads. But, as can here be seen, it is more economic to run a position for the full forward period and quite possibly benefit from a fuller application of the original logic behind the trading decision.

Although spread firms are bookmakers and act against you when quoting (i.e. they do not deal on your behalf at best), I reckon that it is much wiser to approach them with an unequivocal statement as to whether you wish to go long or short and then let them work the order in the market. That way, the bargain can be seen as executed at market and therefore the spread firm's profit margin can be understood and controlled to the advantage of the investor.

As matters stand, the Revenue do not seek to tax gains made by investors at spread betting firms in respect of either income or capital. For various reasons I think this is unlikely to change in the foreseeable future - not the least of which is that almost all investors at spread betting firms lose and would, were they liable to taxation, seek loss relief for taxation.

Dealing on SETS

At the time of writing, London is still in transition from market-maker stocks to SETS (where, incidentally, large lines of stock are still typically dealt off the SETS board and through market-makers). This has confused investors who think the spread nakedly proposed by the SETS order board is the spread to accept. It nearly invariably is not save in major stocks where thick and fast dealing is the order of the day as soon as the market opens at 8.00 a.m. Investors should wait until at least 9.30 a.m. before even contemplating the spread shown by the SETS board.

Availability of stock to borrow

It may seem obvious if thus stated but the fact is that lack of availability of stock to borrow is an indicator that a stock should be short sold. After all, a promoter has as his prime requirement that the stock is at as high a price as possible. It makes sense for the promoter to see his stock placed with private individuals who typically do not lend stock.

Short-selling in North America
All stockmarket operations in North America are highly regulated, in theory. Even so, a considerable number of fraudulent promotions emerge every year which makes me wonder why expenses are incurred by the market-regulation authorities to inhibit them. Of course, there are degrees. The New York Stock Exchange is based on major companies where proper conduct is generally the order of the day. But, by the time you pass on and up to Vancouver, you enter a fairyland of unashamed spoofery. There, deceit is a brazen art form. So much so (I and a few friends blew £250,000 there in 1989) that I dropped a note to the Canadian High Commissioner congratulating him on his country's good fortune through the seemingly perpetual boost to its invisible exports originating from fraudulent promotions. There was no reply.

In the same vein, I recall that a few years ago a disgruntled investor shot dead a fraudulent promoter in the lobby of a Toronto hotel. I expect both parties felt strongly about the matter. Certainly, such an approach constitutes effective regulation to my way of thinking.

It is sobering to reflect that, prior to 1979, investing abroad entailed going through the dollar "premium" pool because exchange control forbade one's buying investment currency at the rate applying to settlement of an international trade. This curious nannying of the citizenry was abolished by Mrs. Thatcher - and quite rightly too in my opinion. The boost to Vancouver sometimes makes me wonder.

Short-selling in North America is as regulated as the other aspects of its markets. The differences from the UK are manifold. For instance, you may only sell short on the "up-tick" - i.e. when the last bargain was at a higher price than that which preceded it. You must put up cash or near cash as collateral. And you will undergo disclosure requirements on short positions. That said, the process is much more ordered and organised than in the UK. You borrow stock and bank interest on funds thereby released from the market. A short position can be run for well over a year. On balance, it seems to me to be a much more mature approach - one that stems from a fundamental absence of any ethical objection to short-selling.

Significance of time in a short position
The argument that time in a short position is unimportant, and that all that matters is the quality of the decision to sell a stock, can be readily rebutted by reducing the proposition to absurdity. For, if time never matters, one has only to sell and immediately buy back. This would be nice for the broker, the market-maker and, of course, HM Government and its stamp duty revenues. But it will not be nice for you. Clearly, time must be allowed to affect the market. Perhaps your sale has been struck ahead of the weekend's press. Perhaps you have decided that in the event of there being no developments by the following Monday, the position will be closed without further review of the relevant factors.

But, normally, you will recognise that the more time that you have the more the price should move your way. Arguably, the only person who might be generally reluctant to keep a position open would be somebody who has misled the market and, fearful of being penalised through sustained buying appearing, banks his turn and departs.

Assuming that you do not think that prices generally or your target's sector will advance, you will seek to buy as much time for your brokerage expended as possible. And, in the UK, that time finishes with buying-in. This is the moment when the administration system formally advises that, whereas it may wish you well, it is simply not interested in having the wheels of commerce clogged by your uncompleted bargain. Buying-in may be deferred by selling for delivery at a later date. This can be up to 25 business days from the trade or T date whereas 5 business days is currently normal. At the time of writing, it is not clear whether disclosing oneself as short through deploying the T + 25 option in this manner justifies purchasing the extra 20 days. A better trade may be to sell T + 23.

Here one's dealer asks for a two way price on T + 23. This raises the possibility in the mind of the market-maker that one is closing a short-sale from two dealing days previously - he may therefore bid you better and not note you as necessarily short. In theory, a market-maker should pay one more for the privilege of paying out 20 days later. In practice, he will not.

Short-selling leaders

It is easy to short-sell FT-SE 100 constituents because there are no problems with marketability. And exceptional examples of recent years have been Polly Peck International and Maxwell Communications Corporation and the Internet boom over-promotions such as Bookham, Baltimore and Autonomy. Sadly, I doubt if we will again get presents like those for many years - those companies were really the product of years of general extension of credit by the investing public and, although memories are short, they are not that short.

At this juncture, I would stress that long-term investment is a form of granting of credit - it is just that the management of the chosen company is given the credit by the investor to look after his funds - the only sanction for the investor is a sale of the shares. The result is that fraudulent conduct within a company can roll up for years or, even, decades. The end result is a much more pronounced fall. The only other point is that all people throughout history have at times and in concert unwittingly extended credit to excess. This phenomenon is known as a "credit boom". It follows that all regulatory measures to inhibit such booms must fail and that any money spent on such measures is money wasted. I would not mind if it were the case that regulators were to pay for themselves and were to remain an optional extra - rather like downmarket after dinner mints. But they do not.

I have digressed. In general, one should not short-sell leaders. The reason is that they are heavily researched and generate sufficient brokerage for really able and prompt institutional brokers to get their large clients out. Put another way, one is unlikely to identify the 20%+ overvaluation that one really ought to have on one's side before proceeding to short-sell.

Over the years, I have occasionally made money on sustained and renewed FT-SE 100 short-sales (I am thinking of Glaxo in the face of Clinton's opening months in the White House). But it can cost something like 15% in expenses in a year and I think it is arrogant at one level and impractical at another to seek to beat the major fund managers by 15% in one year.

Choosing a broker to short-sell for you
Some have argued that, were one able to deal directly with market-makers, one could reduce brokerage costs. And I certainly think that the intelligence of market-makers is frequently overrated - there is undoubtedly scope to beat them at their own game. But, in practice, unless one is conducting a highly controlled and major long fund for a respected fund management concern (where short-selling is, for reasons considered elsewhere, generally and properly banned – unless it is a fund which is authorised to short-sell) it is not possible to deal directly with the market. One must choose a broker.

But there is another reason why a broker is important. He is typically the only person between you and the market and he can (or should be able to) detect when a position is being pressed too hard. Further, such detection will probably be at a moment when markets are moving quickly. So the first requirement of a broker is that he should not be capable of losing his temper and/or judgement under pressure. Surprisingly, not all those licensed as registered representatives have such a disposition. And the philosophical nature required is not normally developed in a broker under the age of thirty. I reckon that as sound a way as any to judge a broker is to take him to lunch. Copious wine soon causes a coarse or inconsiderate fellow to reveal his true self. I may add that, as a gambler, I have tried brokers whom I originally found wanting on this basic lunchtime review. They have proved useless. The cost thus incurred has been considerable.

By and large, institutional brokers work for the larger securities houses. They do not even think of short-selling except in unusual market operations associated with major investment or corporate clients. Thus, although intellectually and emotionally up to speed, they are not available. Your choice must be from a predominantly private client-based firm -

since a discount broker, the only other type of broker, will not knowingly short-sell. Your choice must evidence good time-keeping and sobriety. I do not care whether the claimant has a head of cast-iron; he cannot deal effectively if he is out of his office and/or trying to accommodate half a bottle of gin. Small mistakes, normally overlooked on the long-term long tack, can easily cost a percent or two from time to time. Since the long term trend of markets is to go up with inflation, these small mistakes can be overlooked when they arise on the long tack but they are intolerable on the short-term short tack. This means that your choice should be a sandwiches and water man in the main during dealing hours. I have already admitted that I was not a good broker.

If your broker is any good, he will have made some money personally by the time he is north of thirty years old - both as an investor and from commissions. He will therefore be able to open a £100,000 position without referring to the compliance officers on the point of credit risk. The other type of fellow who is virtually stony-broke through incompetence or failure cannot assist. And, incidentally, one should be suspicious of a broker under the age of thirty who has made a lot of money on his own account - it is quite possible that such money was not made honestly or, if it was, it was made in such a hurry that his equanimity may not be taken for granted.

Further, the fact is that, although almost any broker you might consider or approach is not going to be an intellectual of the first order (because, if he were, he would not be sitting behind a screen), you should not therefore decline to judge the fellow's brain. Say what you will, brainpower helps in every walk of life. There are all sorts of practical tests. Does the chap do *The Times* crossword? Does he convincingly refer to recent and civilising artistic performances? Is he an expert on gardening? Does he prefer Burgundy to Champagne? This last one is quite a good test because you can be in his presence at that very moment. And so on. On the matter of personal qualities, I would run the risk of being mega-boring if I were to list my selection of essentials for clearance - because we all have our own tests that have been gathered through harsh and extensive experience. But one overlooks this review at one's peril. For instance, a broker who criticises people behind their back yet who declines to do so to their face is not merely a coward, he certainly will not speak for you when the going gets tough - as it occasionally does.

Commission payable to a broker - and how to handle him
I doubt if any private investor is wise to negotiate commissions down to below 0.3%. Indeed, such negotiation should be accompanied by assurances of commission of not less than £10,000 p.a. Although it is possible, any saving thus achieved only puts a broker's back up. Personally, I think 0.4% or £40 minimum is fair with (say) £20 as a flat charge to close within 20 business days. I think this entitles one to an enthusiastic and creative relationship with the broker and his desk of immediate associates. Apart from immediate settlement of debits the instant they are due and preferably in advance, I think the broker is entitled to be able to speak to you in business hours. There is no substitute for a direct line to your desk. Unless severely controlled, this facility can be intrusive into other aspects of your daily life.

But it is wholly unreasonable to disappear for a three-hour lunch leaving your unfortunate broker unable to proceed during fast moving markets and then to expect the best results from him. Do not forget that he, for his part, has to be on parade since well before 8.00 a.m. and cannot knock off until 4.30 p.m. or, frequently, later. It is not best practice to make the fellow nervous. It follows that a holiday of more than two business days, particularly where one may not be reached by telephone, is usually best preceded by the closing down of all positions. This means, of course, that no new positions should be opened for some weeks before one goes on holiday. In turn, this may mean no commission for the broker. But the alternative can be tears. I know a broker who went on holiday leaving his clerk to cope with exceptional 10% daily movements in the FT-SE 100 index. When the broker got back there was a bad debt of £1,500,000 to contemplate. I am tolerably sure that this put a dampener on his recollection of the holiday.

It is also important to tell your broker that you are short-selling before you place a sell order. This means that the bargain is booked into a controlled "bear" account allowing your broker to calculate his position at all times. If you do not advise that you are short-selling, the broker will invariably shortly find out and question your every move thereafter. It follows that your broker must work for a firm that will allow short-sales. By no means all firms do.

Internet dealing is different since no service is rendered by mechanised dealing services other than basic execution. Here brokerage can go as low as 0.1%.

It is not a case of my being bloody-minded but I decline to take margin calls before 10.00 a.m. This is partly because the Book Of The Week on Radio 4 is not over until then but principally because prices have not settled down and any decision to trade simply by way of complying with margin requirements is necessarily flawed.

Collateral

Collateral is almost always sought by brokers acting for short-sellers. A rule of thumb is that 30% by way of deemed value of the outstanding position as ameliorated by unrealised profits or increased by unrealised losses will be sought. So, if you are short of £100,000 of stock, you must have £30,000 with your broker and stand prepared to put up £1.30 for every pound the position goes against you. Cash as collateral is not essential for some brokers. Stock registered in his nominee will do. If it is marketable stock, it may be accepted as collateral up to 80% of its bid value. If it is less marketable stock or spread over few holdings or merely confined to one holding, then the rules can be tightened. And they will be tightened unilaterally by people who cannot profit if you succeed and who may lose their job if you fail.

The result is that, when the going gets tough, you need not look to the administrators or regulators for assistance. They are indifferent to past commissions achieved on your account. The only cure is to keep a very healthy collateral position to hand. Interestingly, I have never succeeded in arguing that a number of short positions tend to render the aggregate exposure in line with the volatility of the market in general and that a reduced collateral requirement should therefore suffice. Further, I have never successfully argued to a broker (he faces problems from the regulators) that short positions will tend to reduce the risk of losing on one's long positions. Of course, one could not advance such an argument where the short positions had come to exceed the long positions or where the volatility profiles of the shorts materially exceeded that of the longs.

Bargain sizes

It is common sense to recognise that however precise and astute one's judgement may be, dealing costs must always be seen as a percentage. Quite simply, minimum brokerage of (say) £25 to open and £25 to close, in addition to 0.5% stamp duty, can add up on a bargain of the order of £1,000 to about 6%. And if a regulator adds on a compliance fee of a further £7.50 (a compliance fee is a charge for being honest and competent - which I have always thought the brokerage firm should be to start with) on each bargain the percentage rapidly rises to about 7%. To beat the market by 7% in a few weeks takes exceptional skill or luck. And those who rely upon luck alone soon get wiped out. The only cure is to increase the bargain size to the point where the round turn brokerage and stamp duty expenses total together under 3% and preferably 2%.

Of course, I have only hitherto considered expenses that one incurs through a broker. No filing system ever paid for itself. Time, even one's own, is not for free. And although the best means of recovering one's own time and administration costs is more and more good ideas, one should never forget that all costs must be seen in perspective at all times.
The other cost arising from using the market is the market-maker's "turn". I do not know how much this is. In the mad days of mid- to late-1987, one could frequently buy and sell simultaneously at around the same price in quite a number of stocks. In that sense, market-makers made no charge to speak of.

Then the October 1987 crash came and margins instantly widened as competition in pricing dropped away through the losses and nervousness of the market-makers. I would love to see the current management accounts of the likes of Merrill Lynch (MLSB) or Winterflood Securities

(WINS) - to name two well known market-makers, particularly in respect of that latter firm's position in smaller stocks. I would be very surprised to learn that the profit on turnover in smaller stocks is on average less than 1%. And, given that the FSA thinks that the average profit on turnover in all stocks is 0.75%, I guess that it is probably a lot more, particularly with the smallest and least liquid stocks (I consider a typical example in the next paragraph).

Of course, a fiction of service to the public available at the LSE is that where there is in effect (or as overtly stated) only one market-maker, there is scope to trade on the short tack. This fiction is absurd and inefficient. And, en passant, it is not that attractive on the long tack either. However, and setting aside this declaration of personal displeasure, the moral is clear: you must confine yourself to trading stocks where there are at least two market-makers dealing in your chosen bargain size or more. If you break this rule, market-makers will see you coming and show you no mercy. They are only in the game to profit at your expense.

Buying-in: cause and avoidance

If one fails to deliver stock within five business days of it being sold, the central clearing house of the LSE can first give you notice that it will buy you in and, then, after no delivery, that is exactly what it will do. It makes a charge of £20 for each day of deemed default (nice work if you can get it). But, in practice, the threat of buying-in takes much longer than merely passing the agreed or bargain delivery date. So one has some room - although there is no guarantee of it.

In 1990 to 1991, when Goldman Sachs was closely associated with Robert Maxwell, that firm's market-making arm was usually the best bid for stock (for reasons of contract that were only disclosed later) and so received the normal long and short-sales of Maxwell Communication Corporation stock. However, when investors missed account day for settlement by delivery of stock, Goldman Sachs compelled cash purchases to cover delivery of stock - this was frequently at a higher price than the normal offer price (one would normally expect a cash discount when paying cash). You have been warned - exceptional circumstances can return. Although I have always assumed that the LSE's buying-in office does not disclose the fact of short-sold stock (as indicated by frequent and substantial delays in delivery), the market eventually notes that stock is not being delivered.

Occasionally, it puts two and two together. That is also an occasion to avoid. In my experience, the buying-in office do their work fairly and reasonably. But they will buy you in and they will not discuss with you whether they should pay more to do so - this can be suddenly very costly for you. They, on the other hand, are just obeying the rules.

Covering in ADRs

It is sometimes forgotten that, although one might be deterred from taking a strong short position in the UK market because there is only a small "float" of shares, the target company may have issued ADRs (American Depositary Receipts) typically quoted on the NYSE. This means that one can in extremis cover in New York in respect of a UK sale. However, there are a number of drawbacks. Virtually all American stockbrokers are difficult to deal with unless you trade with them frequently. As a result, if dealing occasionally, one has to treat them carefully and cautiously. This is exhausting if one is accustomed to dealing with one's British broker in a courteous fashion.

For instance, one should never deal with an American broker unless one has a clear agreement in advance of dealing as to the commission to be charged. As one well-known UK market dealer once told me "the value of goodwill ascribable to an American stockbroking firm is twenty-four hours commission". I suppose he should have added "as reduced by provisions for the cost of litigation arising from the dereliction of employees now departed". Strangely, this will still give a positive value despite litigation being extensively in prospect! But, that hurdle aside, you then face five business days before settlement in US dollars and, then, a delay of about a week when convening the ADRs to UK stock ready for delivery. Typically the cost of this conversion is about 5% and arises because the New York ADR official holder/registrar faces no competition in the UK when asked to effect the conversion. That said, you cannot be backed into a corner simply as a consequence of the UK technical supply position. It helps if you are based in London so that couriers may be deployed and controlled to ensure that no delays occur such that one is bought-in in London before one has had an opportunity to deliver. I have, of course, here set out a reserve tactic if the London market looks particularly squeezy. It stops one having to rely on London market makers getting round to arbitraging between London and New York.

One must appreciate that US brokers are quite different to their UK counterparts. Absolutely any old lie will be wheeled on to support their line of bullshit and/or outright theft. US brokers have absolutely no sense of shame. They particularly prove this when dealing with overseas clients. For instance a friend of mine left $300,000 in his account uninvested and untouched for some months only to return from a long trip to find that a contract note for stock whose purchase he had never authorised. Needless to add the stock was by then virtually valueless and it had been stuck on my friend's account by the US broker while my friend was away. The contract note was sent to the correct address save that the country was declared to be Germany rather than Belgium – so to achieve postal delays. The US broker's compliance officer has so far simply asserted that my friend must have placed the order when it is absolutely inconceivable that he could have at the time claimed. Fortunately this sort of thing does not go on in the UK.

Handling positions in the light of press/other commentary

Even experienced short-sellers sometimes forget that for every sale they transact there must be a corresponding purchase. And, after the sale, there must be other sellers to follow - the price will most probably not otherwise decline. The consequence of the first point is that the short-seller must be modest enough to realise that he could be misinformed. It is not therefore wise to keep selling just because the price has gone down or seems to have broken a chart point. The fact is that the bulk of one's selling should be done at the start of a short-term decline. Similarly, if a stock has been lambasted in (say) a week of press comment followed by another dose in the weekend press, the chances of being well advised to sell on the following Monday are very slight because all the short-term selling that can occur has occurred. It is therefore foolish and irrelevant to regard the fundamental case for selling on such a Monday as so strong as to be able to override the fact that selling by others will not occur after you have made the proposed Monday sale. To be sure, after the inevitable "dead cat" bounce/recovery as "bargain hunters" and short-sale closers buy, a fresh opportunity to sell will present itself. This is particularly true if the company comes out with some totally ridiculous statement to reassure investors.

You can usually tell when such a statement is ridiculous because the tone is wrong. The one I like best is the company's advice that "at this level, we are bound to be bid for". No company in history has ever been sensibly offered for sale in this manner. Therefore, such a remark is a declaration of open season. There are hundreds of variations of the informative remarks/ announcements syndrome. You just pick them up as you go along. For instance, the news that Martha Lane-Fox of Lastminute.com had bought 25,000 shares at 39p (when the company had previously not denied press speculation that it was considering an MBO at 90p) is no great vote of confidence. The blue-blooded Lane-Fox's could afford a lot more than £10,000 if they really believed the story.

In recent times, I particularly liked the announcement that Independent Insurance Group would be seeking a rights issue or a takeover when it was obvious that it had been trying to get a rights issue away for weeks and had failed since it had not been possible to quantify liabilities for the sake of the prospectus. This of course also meant that there could be no takeover since what bidder would pay any cash for an insurance company whose liabilities were not quantified. It was possible to keep selling Independent after this announcement and this is as good an example of being invited to a funeral by the prospective deceased as I have ever encountered. Independent was a big payday for Cawkwell Inc.

Setting closing bargains against open positions
Quite possibly, a short-seller may increase his short position a few days after the original sale before any question of his being compelled to buy to close the first sale. Then, rather than his awaiting being compelled to buy to close, he elects to do just that. Frequently, he has the option of setting

this first closing bargain against the second sale - of course, he might not wish to do so on the grounds that, since he has incurred the expense of opening the second position, he would wish to run it as long as possible. But, and nonetheless, he may prefer to set the closing bargain against the second sale because the profit is greater and he would prefer the cash sooner. It is a small point. But in the short-selling game economy and versatility are essential.

Meeting dividend claims; some reflections upon Capital Gains Tax (CGT)

For many years, short-sellers could find a short-sold stock going ex-dividend prior to their closing. A debit would appear on one's statement months, perhaps many months, after one had bought to close The happiest position arose - and still does arise - when the dividend was cancelled through a change of heart on the part of the company: closing bargains struck at the "ex-div" price stand and are not amended upwards. But the debit was only the net dividend. The national income figures were swollen to an extent by dividends that were never actually paid! Nowadays, although one is debited with not only the net dividend but, also, the related tax, the curious statistical effect remains. The tax just makes things a little more costly. Incidentally, it is interesting to note that the CGT legislation gives tax relief on the gross cost of dividends claimed - this gross cost is added on to the cost to close. There is no CGT indexation relief on the cost since the stock is not deemed to have been held for the minimum period required for indexation -this is despite the fact that inflation must work against the short-seller.

Stamp duty

In practice, barring use of Contracts for Differences and spread betting, it is not possible for the private investor to avoid stamp duty on UK equities (excepting when they are purchased in ADR form) when buying to close. Given that stamp duty is a cost of acquisition, it is a little odd that one can be taxed on the purchase of something one never had and where a purchase is simply to close a short-sale. I think the short answer is that stamp duty is not a tax on the fact of acquisition. It is in fact a tax on a document. That, as they say, is as may be. Government pronouncements have tantalised investors with the prospect of nil stamp duty. Indeed, such nirvana was promised if the LSE had been able to come up with an improved stock registration and bargain handling system.

The project was known as Taurus. Its eventual abortion cost the market about £300m and stamp duty remains. I doubt if stamp duty will ever go unless the market is so depressed that capital raising demands that markets are stimulated by the elimination of stamp duty.

"Cashing and renewing": how it occurs and its converse, "renewing and cashing"; widening spreads on"renewing and cashing"

There was a time when stamp duty was refunded if a position was closed within the LSE account. That time was followed by the years 1986 to 1994 (in July 1994, account trading ceased) when stamp duty was not refunded on an account trade. However, under both regimes, buyers faced the requirement to settle on the settlement day for that particular account. Since that entailed putting up cash, some investors simultaneously sold in the current account and bought back their position for the new account and, because the bargains were matched, the market-maker's turn, although most certainly there, was less than the "touch". There was also an imputed charge for the market-maker to finance the position. The effective rate of interest was outrageous and that was true whether the stamp duty was refunded or not.

 I have some small sympathy with the market-makers - after all, they are entitled to categorise an investor's buy order as speculative and inadequately financed. They are entitled to sell stock in the market generally in the belief that he who has bought speculatively will dump the stock fairly shortly afterwards. If, then, this stock is denied to the market through its being carried over to a later account, the market-maker will find himself short of stock. That said, he doesn't half know that there is a compulsory seller out there.

This process was known as "cashing and newing". The "newing" bit is now redundant because the "new" of "newing" referred to the new account. And there is no more account trading. That said, investors can buy on deferred terms and they may wish to renew their positions. So I suppose that "cashing and newing" will persist. Without wishing to bore everybody, I suppose it could be called "cashing and renewing". It should be noted that about three years ago this "rolling" of positions more than once was banned by the LSE. Of course, the converse of cashing and newing, only encountered by the short-seller, must be known as "renewing and cashing". Given that the market is not financing the stock, the market-maker's dealing turn should be approaching nonexistent. It often is not. Again, there is a curious feature, which arises with the approaching suspension of a quotation. If this is seen as likely, the market-makers appreciate that those seeking to "renew and cash" stand to make a lot of money. Therefore, the market-makers tend to widen their dealing turn on the renewal. One would have thought that competition would inhibit this process. But it does not. In their defence, once suspension has occurred, your broker becomes their counterparty and thus, under the minimum capital requirements with which all professionals in the market must cope, capital is absorbed - the widening of spreads is the only way to cope with this problem in advance. The trouble is the extra thus charged is grotesquely excessive when compared with any conceivable discounted cost of risk.

Time/risk exposure
The longer that you stay short, the greater your risk of a major loss. This will sound a strange caveat in the light of my urging you to buy as much time as possible to stay short.

Information comes from all angles
As in life in general, one must always keep an open mind for fresh information. Information on the long-term long tack arrives and should be acted upon without delay. But should you judge that it is sound, you can sit back. You may even go on holiday. However, information on the short-tack can vitally impact with very little notice. It might be on the television news at 10.00 p.m. - too late for newspaper City desks to air the matter properly in the following day's papers. Thus a classic arbitrage of ignorance arises. This arbitrage is immediate.

Information might come from a court case moving unexpectedly against your target. Most people are amazingly slow to evaluate the consequences of judicial decisions. And, once they get round to them, they overreact. It is a tremendous opportunity for the trader. Sadly, some information received from respectable news services is not merely late, it is wrong either in fact or in tone. Although it seems to come with the stamp of authority, it is actually misleading. To react quickly to that is vital. For instance, in late 1993, Automated Security Holdings announced inter alia that it had suffered a £32m exceptional loss. An hour or so later, during which period directors were free to deal and, indeed, bought; the loss was corrected down to £2m. I wish I were in a position to be so casual with a typewriter.

Arbitraging different classes of capital

The opportunity to arbitrage as between different classes of capital rarely arises. Although LSE market-makers are quite extraordinarily overpaid, they rarely let an opportunity slip. So it is difficult for someone who is not a market-maker to benefit - additionally, it will be borne in mind that someone who is not a market-maker faces substantial expenses not faced by the market-maker. But the opportunities do arise and it is both satisfying and worthwhile to spot the moment.

For instance, in November 1993, a small company, NMC had warrants which fell to be converted for the last time by paying a further 16p per share to derive an ordinary then around £1.10. As it happens, I was bullish towards NMC so I bought about 100,000 warrants at around 90p onwards. Warrants tend to become available just before the final conversion date because warrant holders do not have the money to effect the conversion or, if they do, they do not really want to stay on with the fully paid ordinary shares. They regard the approach of the final conversion date as a moment to leave the party. That is how I was supplied. It is also the case that many investors usually regard any proceeds from sales of warrants as pure profit because the warrants that they hold were issued for free earlier in the company's life. It all depends on what you define as free.

Since I was already over invested in NMC - I had 97,500 warrants before this arbitraging started - I tended to keep short-selling NMC ordinary shares to cover the additional warrants that I had purchased. One effect of the warrant purchases was to try and persuade the market that there might be a sustained demand for the ordinary shares. This tended to push up the price of the ordinary shares - which made for a higher price at which I could short-sell the ordinaries. So, not surprisingly, that was the order in which I executed the trades.

In the absence of an imminent conversion date it is generally unwise to try this arbitrage/short-sell strategy. This is because the theoretical tradeable gap does not necessarily close - indeed it is nearly always certain that the time value in the warrant price will not merely inhibit a trade, it will prohibit it. Of course, the bulk of the NMC warrants could not have been delivered by the market in time for me to meet the deadline for conversion (at which point the warrants would have been worthless). So, where I did not hold a certificate, I asked my broker to ask the market to convert the warrants to ordinary shares and to debit me with the subscription of 16p per share. I then completed delivery to cover my short-sold position. It was worth an average 5p per share profit clear of expenses and risk-free. In short, £5,000 for no work at all.

A wholly unexpected bonus arose because as I never took delivery of the bulk of these warrants from the market, I was refunded the stamp duty on their acquisition, about £500. I call that breakfast, lunch and dinner money.

FT-SE 100

As noted elsewhere, it is far too expensive for a holder of equities to sell all of them on the argument that the market is about to decline 10% - and then top up with a few short sales for good measure. He would very probably be wrong about the extent of the fall by the time he has to buy them back. And, even if he were not, his dealing costs would be prodigious. An effective manner of trading on the view that the market is about to decline generally is to buy put options on the FT-SE 100 index or, better, write call options. It is better because the market usually pays more to the writer rather than the purchaser of an option. The transaction costs are low in relation to the exposure sought. For instance, one might purchase an option to sell the FT-SE at 3,000 points four weeks hence for 50 points. Brokerage varies. But you can expect to negotiate a brokerage of 1% or (as in this instance) 0.5 points (there is no stamp duty) - this is one six thousandth of the underlying "stock".

The market-maker's turn might be (only he knows) a further 2 points and brokerage to close (if a closing bargain is struck) is another 0.5 points. All told, 3 points on 3,000 or one thousandth of the underlying "stock" is a tiny fraction of the costs to sell and repurchase a typical FT-SE 100 constituent - those might total between 2% to 3%. Further, where the futures contract is allowed to run to expiry (but see below) there is no brokerage on the closing bargain - this makes a FT-SE 100 trade even cheaper. The trouble is that it is extremely hard to know which way the FT-SE 100 is going.

We have all read how Bernard Baruch called the 1929 collapse almost to a day. We all know that Sir James Goldsmith went 100% liquid just before October 1987. But, for most mortals, such insight is not available. The truth is that the futures market is only traded by well-informed individuals. Thus, it is not possible for the ordinary investor seriously to contemplate anything other than an insurance transaction -whereas, of course, the short-seller short-term trader must take more out of the market than he puts in taking one year with another. That is hard. Indeed, the future often seems to have a life of its own. There are standard adjustments for the future contract's run to expiry in respect of interest foregone (through being in the FT-SE 100 rather than cash) and ex-dividend dates. But the price actually quoted frequently differs by up to 25 points or more from the expected or theoretical futures price. When this happens, one can forecast with some confidence that the cash or underlying stockmarket is about to catch up in whatever direction is prognosticated. For, nowadays, the cash market is wagged by the future - after all, it is so much cheaper to deal in the future. However, one should be cautious of confident FT-SE 100 forecasts. They are so often wrong.

It is also possible to trade the index as a future. There is the crude daily FTSE quote offered by the spread firms, which I foolishly thought I had come profitably to understand. But the spread is too wide and only works as a tool if one has the very best information – for instance one might note a 1% rise in HK at, say, 7.30 a.m. in the course of a particular minute. Not all spread firms adjust their London FTSE quote sufficiently to recognise that change. I understand that at least one trader has been denied a spread betting facility on daily FTSE simply because the spread firm in question reckoned that it could not compete with this trader's speed of reaction to price-sensitive news. However, it has quite happily trousered £50,000 that I lost on FTSE spread-betting.

An interesting feature of FT-SE 100 trading is that it is settled by reference to a make-up figure which is determined by noting the best bid and the best offer in each FT-SE 100 constituent at the end of each minute from 10.10 a.m. to 10.30 a.m. on the monthly expiry day. This is intended to give an average figure which is difficult to manipulate and which may thus be relied upon. However, the futures market is dominated by market-makers. And they are well aware of their opportunity and sometimes their compelling requirement to hold the market up or force it down in the run-up to and during the final twenty minutes of trading which determine the make-up figure.

It may be wondered how they can do this. Quite simply, one firm might have an exposure of £1 million a FT-SE 100 point. A 25 point movement will cost £25 million. It pays mightily for it to bid up for stock or offer stock in FT-SE 100 constituents in the twenty minutes - depending upon which way its book is suited. Because the trade in the underlying constituents in the FT-SE 100 (as has been noted above) is frequently so thin, it is quite possible to affect the underlying FT-SE 100 average without incurring substantial losses when squaring the positions taken between 10.10 a.m. and 10.30 a.m. For, although market-makers in FT-SE 100 constituents are obliged to deal at the prices shown on their screens and in certain minimum sizes, it will be found that, during the final minutes to the settlement of the make-up of the FT-SE 100, the market-making firm that is engaged in manipulation is curiously reluctant to answer its telephones. Of course, as soon as 10.30 a.m. has come and gone, they are open to all and sundry.

One reason why I advise the typical equities trader not to trade the FT-SE 100 is that the best FT-SE 100 trader of whom I am aware never trades equities. This is because he has decided that he can trade one or the other market but not both. In his opinion, the concentration required in respect of one sector of the market precludes concentrating on the other. He has chosen the FT-SE 100 and he spends something like £50,000 p.a. on information services alone. He holidays for a quarter of the year. But, when trading, he never leaves his desk except to answer the call of nature - and even when thus ensconced he is surrounded by telephones. Unless you are prepared to be as dedicated as that, you should think very carefully about trading the FT-SE 100 with a view to profit as a trader rather than merely insuring your portfolio.

SHORT SELLERS OUT
ON A BEAR RAID

Definition of bear-raiding: S47 and defamation

There is some confusion over the meaning of the term "bear-raid". Simply selling a stock short does not constitute initiating or participating in a bear-raid. Bear-raiding occurs when the short-seller, having sold first, persuades others to sell after him so that the price goes down sufficiently to secure a profit for the first seller. The means of persuasion are varied. For those who are indifferent to lying, a simple lie to another dealer with whom one wishes to get even or merely "rot up" can work. But a story in the press takes more effort and should be more effective.

As it happens, I lie much less often than other people in general. And it also seems to me that lying is an inherent part of the human condition. This creates difficulties at the margin for people who are unable to be philosophical or who do not know their place. But whether all the foregoing is so or not, one point is certain: the law now precludes misleading statements and practices in relation to the stockmarket. This is regulated by the Financial Services Act 1986 and, as of late 2001, the Financial Services and Markets Act 2000. As recounted elsewhere it can lead to a prosecution.

Another problem that can arise is to be on the receiving end of a writ for defamation. Although it is commonly supposed that only people can be defamed whereas companies cannot because companies do not have feelings, companies have legitimate commercial interests. To spread the rumour that Squeaky Clean PLC is questionable when, in fact, it is squeaky clean, is not merely unfair, it is actionable. Even if the plaintiff has no merit, a foolish bear-raider can face substantial legal expenses. I think current defamation law unduly favours fraudsters.

I have mentioned Minmet already. These days I decline to call the management of Minmet PLC anything rude. For, were I to do so, I would simply invite a defamation action. But for the record, my previous column merely highlighted the overvaluation of that company in 2000. The effect was the receipt by the Internet site of a letter from Minmet's lawyers claiming damages and saying that the directors' feelings were hurt. Well, I never did... the poor deary diddums.

These defamation lawyers claimed damages of the order of £25m - lawyers never blush. But I am told that the largest sum ever awarded in favour of a company rather than an individual is £100,000. So as a general rule one should treat these lawyers with derision. The only unfair aspect of their conduct is that whenever they engage in it there is no penalty against them for wasting one's time.

The only other lawyer attack I have experienced was over Helphire where I nearly made a major error. A trade magazine of the insurance industry ran a story in 2000 to the effect that Helphire's business was fatally flawed in that even had their case legal been properly prepared (it evidently had not) the judge's summary (helpfully provided by the trade magazine) seemed to state that in law alone Helphire's claim was unsound. I published accordingly.

Helphire went ballistic and their then brokers Williams de Broe invited me to lunch at their premises in Broadgate to meet the company. Jo Nally of de Broe welcomed me to sit down to the hors d'oeuvre with the news that a well known institutional investor had sent his regards and that the price of Helphire was up from 260p to 350p. Since I was short of 150,000, a sensitive soul would have gagged slightly. But even I was a little concerned to learn that the judge's summary had been revised and that all I had read was a draft judgement.

But here I got lucky. I got hold a of barrister pal, who said that the revised judgment did not affect the conclusions that I had already made and published. That was a relief.

It was some weeks before the judgement of the Appeal Court came up on the Internet (an invaluable service of which I had been unaware at the time – I was thus unable to understand Helphire's melting share price that morning). I banked the money - but not before the usual pile of piffle from the lawyers. And I resent this since each time the pile emerges the publisher gets zonked with a bill for £1,500. And, of course, never an apology from either the lawyer or his client.

Oddly, as I write (two years later) it appears that Helphire might finally be winning its legal battle. But for those two years this has been a shorters dream.

Insider trading and the Financial Services and Markets Act 2000
This book does not offer the opportunity to consider the present law in relation to insider trading. Suffice it to remark that the Government has so hopelessly misunderstood this subject (and over many years) that the chances of common sense being brought to bear are negligible in the foreseeable future. However, clearly, anybody who deals in shares without inside information (in the sense of information not generally appreciated by the market) is, as a French market speculator of late Victorian vintage once remarked, as stupid as he who buys cattle by moonlight. Further, I am attracted to the reform that it should be obligatory to deal only when in possession in fact or by claim of inside information. It would save so much trouble - not least the marketing of hypocrisy by fools, this time posing as regulators, pompously hectoring and deceiving a weary world. But the short-seller is a frequent trader and since his style of trading will eventually throw up a major gain (in absolute or percentage terms) he can

be caught by the law. And the way things are going, somebody is bound to be fingered when entirely innocent.

The unswerving advice here offered is to say absolutely nothing to anybody. Regulators are sometimes people who have failed in their business or in life in general (because, if one stops for two seconds to think about it, it is obvious that nobody would choose to be a eunuch if he could also be the proprietor of the harem). As a result of their inferiority, they seek to pester others so that they can seem important. Further, the law actively encourages and empowers them so to behave. So discretion is your friend.

What may strike you as a chance and irrelevant reflection upon the success of a trade can be taken as potentially incriminating either directly by a regulator or through the agency of betrayal by someone whose livelihood is determined by a regulator. The eventual upshot may well be your acquittal. But the cost is worry and delay. However much you may hold the insider trading law in contempt, the power rests with those who implement it and you challenge that at your peril. With a bit of luck, this state of affairs should not continue forever. At least, I hope not. I also reckon that telephone-tapping by Government is on the way as an officially if clandestinely condoned means of reviewing traders' conduct. So watch your mouth. And, as for your pen, confine it to love letters and history in the public domain. Although England used to be an agreeable country in which to live, simply yearning for a return to carefree days will not bring them back.

Finally, I have traditionally blamed the Conservatives for the absurd panoply of law which now attends the stock market but the Conservatives are dead and gone and their successors, New Labour (the modern version of the Conservatives), have had long enough to continue the meddlesome traditions of their predecessors. This has meant that the Financial Services Act of 1986 has been supplanted by the Financial Services and Markets Act of 2000. I reproduce S118 of that Act. It will be no laughing matter in practice.

PART VIII

PENALTIES FOR MARKET ABUSE

Market abuse

118.—(1) For the purposes of this Act, market abuse is behaviour   Market abuse.
(whether by one person alone or by two or more persons jointly or in
concert)—

- (a) which occurs in relation to qualifying investments traded on a
  market to which this section applies;

- (b) which satisfies any one or more of the conditions set out in
  subsection (2); and

- (c) which is likely to be regarded by a regular user of that market
  who is aware of the behaviour as a failure on the part of the
  person or persons concerned to observe the standard of
  behaviour reasonably expected of a person in his or their
  position in relation to the market.

(2) The conditions are that—

- (a) the behaviour is based on information which is not generally
  available to those using the market but which, if available to a
  regular user of the market, would or would be likely to be
  regarded by him as relevant when deciding the terms on which
  transactions in investments of the kind in question should be
  effected;

- (b) the behaviour is likely to give a regular user of the market a false
  or misleading impression as to the supply of, or demand for, or
  as to the price or value of, investments of the kind in question;

- (c) a regular user of the market would, or would be likely to, regard
  the behaviour as behaviour which would, or would be likely to,
  distort the market in investments of the kind in question.

(3) The Treasury may by order prescribe (whether by name or by description)—

    (a) the markets to which this section applies; and

    (b) the investments which are qualifying investments in relation to those markets.

(4) The order may prescribe different investments or descriptions of investment in relation to different markets or descriptions of market.

(5) Behaviour is to be disregarded for the purposes of subsection (1) unless it occurs—

    (a) in the United Kingdom; or

    (b) in relation to qualifying investments traded on a market to which this section applies which is situated in the United Kingdom or which is accessible electronically in the United Kingdom.

(6) For the purposes of this section, the behaviour which is to be regarded as occurring in relation to qualifying investments includes behaviour which—

    (a) occurs in relation to anything which is the subject matter, or whose price or value is expressed by reference to the price or value, of those qualifying investments; or

    (b) occurs in relation to investments (whether qualifying or not) whose subject matter is those qualifying investments.

(7) Information which can be obtained by research or analysis conducted by, or on behalf of, users of a market is to be regarded for the purposes of this section as being generally available to them.

(8) Behaviour does not amount to market abuse if it conforms with a rule which includes a provision to the effect that behaviour conforming with the rule does not amount to market abuse.

(9) Any reference in this Act to a person engaged in market abuse is a reference to a person engaged in market abuse whether alone or with one or more other persons.

(10) In this section—

    "behaviour" includes action or inaction;

    "investment" is to be read with section 22 and Schedule 2;

    "regular user", in relation to a particular market, means a reasonable person who regularly deals on that market in investments of the kind in question.

GOING LONG!

"A fool ...is a man who never tried an experiment in his life"
-Erasmus Darwin, 1792

Although my main interest lies in short-selling, I have taken the
opportunity here to set out my views about investing for the long term.
Many will think my attitude fairly staid – save with respect to mining
stocks.

Constructing a Sensible Portfolio

Everybody has their own views on what to hold in a portfolio and you
do not have to agree with what I say. But, although I make my money
in the main on fairly short term operations which might most properly
be considered trading rather than investment, I have always taken what I
regard as long term views on equities and am quite prepared to sit there
until I am proved right. The key is insisting on basic criteria being met and
refusing to budge from them.

However, here I wish to commit heresy. About five years ago Jim Slater
launched his REFS investment service on to the investment world. It was
and remains a brilliant achievement. It was accompanied by a method of
selecting growth stocks, partly using REFS but also using eleven sieves,
which I reproduce now:

- A positive growth rate in Earnings Per Share (EPS) in at least four
  of the last five years.
- A low Price Earnings Ratio (PER) relative to growth rate (the
  PEG).
- An optimistic statement from the chairman
- Strong liquidity, low borrowings and high cash flow.
- A substantial competitive advantage.
- Something new.
- A small market capitalisation.
- High relative strength performance of share price.
- A better than nominal dividend yield.

- A reasonable asset position.
- Management should have a significant shareholding, which is not reducing.

That said, sound as this approach is (and I know that Jim himself has made a fortune out of the practical personal application of it), I think it is really intended for bull markets. It is only in bull markets (which he would stress occur most of the time) that it really works.

For myself I like investments that may be a little more pedestrian but which I think have failsafe qualities allowing them to be held with confidence until the truth emerges. I insist on rich asset backing, a strongly solvent position and a recognisable trade. There is absolutely no point in departing from these criteria since, although there are many other good investments, which do not demonstrate these criteria, why risk disappointment? Why not let time be your friend? Asset backing, properly managed, will always come through. Where I am entirely in agreement with Jim is on the need to cut losers. As soon as something goes wrong in a company, sell it. Nine times out of ten, bad news is followed by more bad news.

My biggest mistakes are when I hold on too long. Listeners to my EvilCasts on t1ps.com will by now be used to me saying about once a quarter "I'm a fathead – that's it." When I break my own rules I lose money and swear that I will never do so again. Until the next time.

HEIGH-HO MINING CO.
BOARD OF DIRECTORS

Mining Stocks

I like playing mining stocks on the long tack and have done extremely
well out of them. The Australian mining boom of 1969/70 was my
introduction to lunatic markets of any description and I have never
really lost the taste for mining shares. And, as it happens, 1971 saw me
ensconced as forecast accountant for the nationalised Roan Selection Trust
copper mining assets in Zambia.

This was an interesting assignment since Zambia is the only country of
which I am aware in the world where gambling debts are enforceable by
law (in the Far East they are enforced by violence where necessary). I won
about £3,000 (perhaps £30,000 today) from a local Greek bookmaker who
declined to pay out since he claimed that there was a palpable error in his
pricing the Henry Cecil-trained winner at 12/1 against rather than 2/1
against. I maintained that there was no such error. He had merely read his
telexed information service too literally and knew nothing about English
racing form and could not therefore check the inherently silly proposition

that Cecil would run a three year old handicapper at Newbury where the chance of a win was so lowly rated as to give a 12/1 against price.

A solicitor dealt with the matter expeditiously and effectively. I remain convinced that this bookmaker had been cocky too many times towards his local compatriots and, as a result, when he turned to them for their comments on my claim was advised that settling immediately was the proper way forward. For myself, I would like to have defended his case – but then I like argument even to my own disadvantage.

My time in Zambia was extremely happy – my wife and I were married in Lusaka in 1969 – and we returned to London in 1973. Unfortunately, a sort of democracy rules in Zambia and, as a consequence, the place has become a dump. This is not a PC view so it is worth repeating.

In my role of forecast accountant at RST, I improved my crossword technique. I think that one only ever improves it, since, and as I have earlier remarked, if one were able to do crosswords straight off, one would never bother. Put another way, crosswords are for failures. However, I took time off from the crossword to visit RST's remarkable underground copper mine at Mufulira. This colossal enterprise had a brightly illuminated cathedral-sized cavern hewn from the rock some 2,500 feet below surface and which housed the winding engines for the lifts. It was an awesome sight. Low loaders descended by a spiral roadway all 2,500 feet to the mining face and when we were there were extracting vast loads of bornite which I am told is 70% copper. The price of copper was then sufficient to pay for a new low loader, then about USD 50,000, in ten days. As I say, it was a colossal enterprise.

The interesting feature of our visit was that the mine captain, a bluff and enthusiastic Yorkshireman, drew our attention to the fact that the night before some grass had been found 2,500 feet down and that they were blocking off this fall. Nine days later, there was indeed a further ingress of water, mud and grass (grass only occurs on the surface) from the tailings dambo or lake. About 200 men were drowned. It was many years before Mufulira was back to full operational efficiency.

One conclusion I drew was that miners are a hardy breed. But I am afraid to say that mining also attracts some right little rotters who would never dream of getting their hands dirty. They are some of the promoters of mining stocks. And one really has to keep an eye on them. Which I did not when entertaining such a promoter about twelve years ago. He used make up. I do not think he was effeminate. I think he was just trying to recapture the good looks of his youth. In short, he was not realistic. Where he was especially unrealistic, perhaps fraudulently so, was in failing to secure his oil exploration company's licence rights in Bangladesh. This had the effect of his company having no title to the vast gas strike it paid for and encountered. I suppose he revisited the prospect by a different corporate vehicle later when all the development work had earlier been paid by me and other hapless shareholders. Well, one learns.

Undoubtedly the most striking fraudulent mining promotion in recent years has been Bre-X, a gold mining development company operating under licence in Indonesia. Again, the mine was a long way off and deep in the jungle which restricted visits from shareholders. That said, a friend of mine, charged with buying Bre-X for his company, one of the North American gold majors, was ready to send in geologists to prepare an independent report – after all, his company were to lay out $3 billion for the company – only to find that it was never possible to gain access to the site. The collapse of Bre-X bust hundreds including one major Canadian broker which had allowed many of its clients to buy Bre-X on margin. That was not an intelligent lending operation.

Leaving frauds aside, I think that there is one cardinal principle of a mining investment which is to get it young – i.e. before the public has latched on to its charms. Provided this is done in a bull market for mining stocks (quite often this is when all other sectors are performing badly or indifferently), the gravy is usually yours. Do not hesitate to trade them. Be prepared to build an opening position and to flip out at least half on the major surges and then to reacquire stock as the dip seems to be bottoming out. Unless you know it is a fraud, do not short mining stocks. You simply do not know how far the bull tack will go.

When the frenzy looks to you to have hit its maximum, bail out. Do not return to the stock for at least five years and, even then, remember that successful mining stocks very rarely develop a second life.

Portfolio Spread

First, it is probably unwise to own more than ten stocks. This is easily proved (remember, you are not an institution and you do not have vast quantities of cash which have to be invested over a wide range of equities simply to meet trustees' requirements – many of which seem to me to be impractical or silly). Why would you select an eleventh stock when you selected a first stock as your absolutely best investment and then invested in your second best and so forth? Surely, by the time you get to the tenth, you would only be investing 1% of your portfolio – I assume that you put 40% into the first, 25% into the second, and so forth. It just would not be worth selecting an eleventh. I would here mention that the late unlamented Prime Minister, Harold Wilson, was quite clever and, on his retirement from politics (an event for which we were all truly grateful), chaired a royal commission into capital markets. Evidence was there taken that it was not necessary to hold more than twenty stocks in FTSE to have a very fair chance of matching FTSE's performance. So the argument that one needs lots of investments simply to cut down on volatility is not sound.

The key to success is to be quite ruthless in handling your largest investment. If it underperforms, either by triggering stop losses or missing forecasts, cut it. This ruthlessness is possessed by very few investors and its absence is the biggest single cause of stock market losses. Almost all private investors prefer to take profits and run losses. This practice cannot be supported and clearly arises from deep psychological urges. But I am afreud I am not Freud and cannot help you as to what they are.

Of course, as soon as you have chopped your first investment it follows that your second investment becomes your first investment and it is easier to be ruthless on your second investment than on your first. From there on it is easy to cull. Well, given that I think that it is far harder to sell an equity than to buy one, we have dealt with the hardest part first. Now let us turn to the easy task of stock selection.

Given that there are literally thousands of equities from which to select there is no need to hurry. In fact, I suggest that a novice laying out his first portfolio should decide to buy only one stock in the first three months of his deciding to run his own portfolio. This takes self-control but it causes the investor to be very careful. The second investment might come not less than three months after the first. But do invest 40% of your fund in your best investment. Life is not a rehearsal.

Markets Do Not Travel in a Straight Line

I find it constitutionally difficult to take a profit. As a result as a stock goes to new highs or, more typically as far as I am concerned, new lows, I do not take profits. This can be unwise since the fact is that there are always technical reactions in the pipeline – and sometimes they can be very vicious. I put this in simply to warn the reader not to be as silly as I have occasionally proved to have been. Losing £750,000 in the three weeks after September 21st 2001 was – as I admitted to t1ps.com listeners – very foolish. It meant that my profit on the year was only £500,000. Vintners across the capital were devastated.

Indices

Stock indices have been around for some time. They started off giving a general guide to the level of prices but by 1935 more attention to weighting and representation offered the UK the FT 30 index. It was entirely made up of industrials and excluded retailers, banks and mines to name just a few sectors that might have been included. It is a measure of how England's national product was then derived and how it has changed. Just guessing, I suppose at the time of writing that the entirety of manufacturing UK, whether quoted or unquoted, is less than the capitalisation of Vodafone alone.

Since I am not a mathematician I decline to continue this commentary for fear of making an egregious blunder. But I would make the general remark that beating the current major London index, FTSE100, is difficult since entrants come in at the valuation of the day they enter and immediately accelerate as index funds take their portion – one can never deal at the entry price on average. It gets worse on the exit. Where a stock precipitates out (Maxwell, Polly Peck), it leaves at the valuation point it enjoyed in the index. However, it is quite impossible to sell on the way out at that valuation.

The effect of all this is that FTSE100 may be of interest but it is extremely hard to outperform it.

That said, dear reader, I have personally massively outperformed FTSE, and any other index you care to name. So I do not personally care that its fundamental flaws in construction – designed to promote the stock exchange on which it is based – apply. Of course, it is helpful when short-selling in that no capital is required such that there is an infinite return on capital employed. (Cash as collateral is not invested – it merely earns interest – those wishing to object to this argument can write to me at Evil Towers and I will file their thoughts in an appropriate place.)

Company Visits

These used to be much easier to arrange – companies, particularly small companies that had no effective broker support, were flattered and delighted to be visited. Nowadays, they are wary of the insider dealing rules and much more cautious as to what they say and to whom. But I still think a visit has much to commend it. A visit gives one a sense of the company's general conduct. I offer two examples:

In 1989, I visited Desoutter in north London since I had heard a rumour of a bid. When I got to its premises, I asked to see the factory in operation. They declined. This was most unusual since – and as I said - companies like to show themselves. I therefore decided that Desoutter was concerned to see that its general level of activity was kept back from public scrutiny and I guessed that that was not because of poor trading. The share price duly doubled three months later.

Another example of a useful company visit was one I made to Marks and Spencers vast head office in Baker Street in 1992 (by way of some business with the late Lord Sieff, then the chairman). I saw huge space occupied by a few directors and a lavish catering staff in attendance. I knew the company was doomed and sold my father's holding at around 650p. Given that the market then doubled whilst the share price halved, I regard that as having been a useful visit. Who would not?

I add a third point. My www.t1ps.com colleague Zak Mir relates that a while back he attempted to interview Arena Leisure – a company whose significant de-rating has significantly boosted the net assets of S. Cawkwell enterprises. Arena declined on a number of occasions to speak to Zak. It strikes me as obvious that if Arena had a good story to tell it would have been delighted to relay it to such an influential chap as Zak. The silence of Arena spoke volumes.

Reading Accounts

Although I have practised as a chartered accountant for more than a quarter of a century, I do not claim to be an expert in accounting standards. This is not because they are uninteresting or difficult to understand. It is because they are constantly changing and never of serious import for the small companies covered by my practice. But one should not make any mistake. Accounts need to be read very carefully. And one starts at the back.

The reason for reading them in reverse is that all managements seek to deceive – either through over promotion of their achievements or prospects or to conceal just how cheap their stock is. So the front pages are the advertising section and the back pages are dedicated to deceiving investors.

Some areas which I know are very rewarding for the discerning investor are:

- Fair value accounting. This is a process whereby a company that is acquired comes with a set of balances in its books, which need amendment in favour of the acquiring company. At that point the acquiring company reassesses what it claims to be the true underlying position and, typically, raises credit balances for costs to come such as reorganisation. The resultant and matching debit balance is charged to goodwill on acquisition account. This is either held in the balance sheet for amortisation over a sensible number of years (well, that is what the directors claim – as aided by the auditors) or it is written off to shareholders funds. This latter move is often adopted when investors are obsessed by earnings per share rather than tangible net asset backing – I hope readers fall in the latter category. Finally, the credit balance is used to absorb expenses in later years which would otherwise be written off to profit and loss account. This allows the management to inflate earnings. The sums involved can be very material.

- Capitalisation of expenses which would normally be written off. A current example is costs associated with landing a sale by Private Finance Initiative companies.
- Variation of accounting policies from one year to the next. Believe it or not this can allow the same contribution to profit to be reported in each of two successive years. A glance at the comparatives appearing in the second set of accounts with the figures originally disclosed can be very rewarding.
- Tax charges: Low tax rates charged suggest that revenue costs for tax have been capitalised. Incidentally, as Tom Winnifrith and I explained on t1ps.com (in a piece that was miraculously picked up by Private Eye shortly afterwards), the companies run by Mr Blair's good friend Mr Mittal benefit from both a low tax charge and also changes in their (very generous) depreciation policies.

Timing of recognition of income.

I do not wish to be thought offensive or cynical but there is no escaping the fact that, sometimes, perfectly sensible auditors of high personal principle get lent on by overwheening managements and, as a result, a true and fair view tends to go by the way. I am sure this happened with Maxwell and I am sure it will happen for all time to come. It is also true that entirely legitimate adoption of accounting standards can lead to distorted accounts for the novice reader. For instance, if a hotel company were to take profit in an accounting period in respect of next year's forward bookings, there would be a computation of the relevant associated costs and the consequences of people not complying with their bookings. In short, not merely would tax be paid on cash that had not yet been received but there would not be that much in it and, as a result, hotel companies do not so account.

But an entirely different state of affairs arose in 1999/2000 when the market was ready to accord walking-on-water status to TMT stocks. It was therefore very attractive for TMT managements to book profits long before the cash would actually be received. After all, the associated costs were relatively slight (profit margins were colossal). If it had not been so booked, the earnings reported would have been negligible or non-existent. The trick in taking the profit earlier lay in the fact that investors could not be bothered to read the accounts of these companies and were therefore prepared to give a stratospheric rating to the companies thus accounted and promoted. I may add that this sort of nonsense is not permitted in the US – all investors can only look at all companies on the basis that a sale has been made and the services or goods delivered.

It was this advance booking of future revenues that proved the undoing of Cedar – one of my big winners of 2001.

Ramping

For some extraordinary reason our legislators cling to the idea that markets should not be "manipulated". I have no idea why they so think or what they mean by the term. And nor do they. They have however devised a term "market abuse" which they see as an activity demanding criminal prosecution. It is set out in S118 of the Financial Services and Markets Act 2000. I now describe activities that are illegal and if offered to you should be promptly dismissed for what they are: self-serving rubbish.

Although it is not generally so recognised, it is a criminal offence to speak to somebody so that it could be argued that advice had been given on investments and where the speaker is not authorised under the relevant legislation so to speak. Further, any losses suffered by the listener pursuant to such advice can theoretically be recovered from the speaker. It should be added that there are evidential problems. So, should you feel aggrieved, I suggest you cool down first.

But the first rule of ramping is not to "hot" women. I am not sure why this is so. But the golden rule of "hot-boxing" (the practice of renting an office in, say Amsterdam, and telephoning soft touches with unique investment opportunities, particularly ones involving sending cheques to box numbers) is not to "pitch the bitch". This is because women really do get worked up about bad advice and consequently take the fact of it up with the authorities. Men might feel tempted so to react but since talking to the authorities inevitably involves declaring that they, the men, are complete fools duck before this effort to be all righteous.

However, there is another class of investor, the members of which are not completely wet behind the ears and who will listen to some fellow who has taken the trouble to telephone him out of the blue with a hot tip. For some reason this class is still able to make an elementary mistake in that it is virtually certain that the speaker is seeking to deceive the listener, There is the confidential cough, the allusion to a claim to know somebody on the inside (this particular line of attack is effective since the listener cannot complain at the consequences of listening because, having dealt on inside information, he also is in breach of the law) and, of course, the reliance on the belief that last week's bad advice will, through the law of averages , be followed by good advice and so on and so forth.

It really does not matter how the proposition is wrapped up; it is nearly always deceptive even if good advice in practice. I have studied this incidence of deception for so long that I now think that all private client stockbroking advice is corrupt since the order in which good advice is disseminated has little or nothing to do with equity and, more interestingly, cannot have.

Quite how citizens are supposed to know this as of birth is beyond me and I here pass on the amusing tale of a young man, Jonathan Lebed, who simply cannot have known that he was in breach of the law. He therefore gets full marks from me for enterprise at an early age.

The tale of Jonathan Lebed is certainly heart-warming. In September 1999, Jonathan, of Cedars Grove High School, Cedars Grove, New Jersey was fourteen years old and had lately received a personal computer. His father, who is not computer literate, subsequently put his son's problems down to the arrival of this computer. Mother's remarks are not recorded but she seems to have had a little more common sense. And, if she did not have that, she certainly left her son to get on with ramping stocks. Needless to add, he only started ramping by accident. It must have seemed to him to be merely a form of playground joshing carried out privately in his bedroom.

He was interested in the stock market since his parents had kept him informed of their modest portfolio. Jonathan watched CNBC and, when he was twelve, got hold of $8,000 from his parents. Over the following year he turned this into $28,000. He observed the Internet bulletin boards had an effect on stock prices and offered a few insertions of his own. Initially, these were rather mild but effective – they were believed and tended to put up prices of stock where Jonathan was long. However, he upgraded them by making them ridiculously emphatic and confident with liberal exclamation marks and sentences interlaced with CAPITALS – just like that. He found that this immoderate style achieved much more significant results. A year later he had made $800,000. But it was then that the SEC took a hand and sought to prosecute him. The SEC is the USA's equivalent of our FSA but run by people who are even more stupid. I know that this must seem technically impossible. However, it is true.

The SEC settled for $280,000 of the profit to be handed back to them to settle the market manipulation charges. But they demonstrated that market manipulation is a rather silly activity to categorise as a crime given that it only thrives through human greed and naivety (two ineradicable features of human life – after all, just why would any reasonable person buy on the uncorroborated and unpaid for advice of an unidentified person?). I think the trouble is that those who regulate stock markets have tried to turn trading on stock markets into a religious activity. Seems a pretty curious choice for a religion to me.

Insider Trading Investigations

These are conducted by the DTI and, I am told, always begin with the question "Do you know Simon Cawkwell?" This is of course flattering if not entirely true since the ones that I personally attend inevitably do not so begin. Unfortunately I cannot tell you which ones I have personally attended since to do so would be a criminal offence. I cannot imagine why – you would really have to take it up with the regulators.

CONCLUSION

"Prudence is a rich, ugly old maid courted by Incapacity."
- William Blake, Proverbs of Hell

Perhaps slightly arrogantly I reckon that a fund manager does not come into his own until he is forty years old. Before that time it is unlikely that anyone will have seen the full cycle of wholesale granting of credit and wholesale withdrawal of all credit. And it is worth remembering that twentieth century Britain only saw two proper bear markets - that of 1929 to 1932 and 1973 to December 1974. Since I am only fifty-five and since I intend to push at fund management for at least another twenty years, I have not yet reached half way through my career. The only inhibitory factor is that since I live so well by fund management I may go pop before I am seventy-five.

Of course, I have run some major risks, which with the benefit of hindsight I should have controlled. For instance, when Tiphook was entering the home straight towards the funeral parlour, I increased my short to 500,000 shares at around 40p. The error that I made was that I did not think that Tiphook's management would have one last gasp effort at imaginative accounting. The result was that on the announcement of one of its last sets of figures to the market the shares jumped to 90p. That made me think. Fortunately, my various brokers knew that it was pointless to upset my equilibrium by advising to me close in whole or in part. So I went for a walk, came back and sold yet more. That eventually came good. But it was a close call. And I should not have pushed my luck that far - however sure I was of my argument.

Undoubtedly my greatest triumph to date has been Maxwell in 1991. It is not that the profit made, £250,000, was all that sensational - I have certainly made (and lost) much more than that in a day. It was that it set me on a way of life knowing that I had pulled off a stroke. I enjoyed that. And I still do.

I sometimes fear that Britain will emerge as a capitalist country where I face reasonable and informed competition. Fortunately, this does not look like proving to be the case.

INDEX

"So essential did I consider an Index to every book, that I proposed to bring a Bill into Parliament to deprive an author who publishes a book without an Index of the priviledge of copywright; and, moreover. to subject him, for his offence, to a pecuniary penalty"

Chief Justice Baron Campbell (1779 - 1861)